I0048881

"This book is a game changer that needs to be read, studied, and talked about by all women in leadership roles—especially in the non-profit sector. *Character Driven Leadership* is more than a leadership book—it's a toolkit for developing a genuine, values-based leadership style."

KIMBERLEY MACKENZIE, CPCC, ACC, charity executive, leadership coach

"*Character Driven Leadership for Women* is perfect for anyone eager to build self-awareness as a foundation for both personal and professional growth. Reading *Character Driven Leadership for Women* left me feeling validated, inspired, and focused—it's essential for anyone ready to break free from autopilot and start leading with intention and purpose."

MICHELLE VELLA, founder, The Tailored Career

"*Character Driven Leadership for Women* is a must-read for anyone interested in empowering the next generation of female leaders. Known as a trusted authority on women's leadership, Kathy Archer combines her deep expertise with powerful insights to challenge conventional leadership norms and promises to change how we view leadership for good in the nonprofit sector."

HALEY COOPER, founder, The Savvy Fundraiser

"*Character Driven Leadership for Women* is a must-read for women nonprofit leaders who want to lead with purpose, integrity, and resilience. Kathy Archer tackles the realities of managing the constant demands of leadership with insights to help us align our actions with our core beliefs. She's been where we are and understands what it takes to grow into the kind of leader we aspire to be—one who leads authentically and effectively."

HEATHER HOOPER, CEO, Heather Hooper Consulting

"*Character Driven Leadership for Women* is the toolkit for people in leadership, especially women who are navigating leadership in nonprofit and values-driven spaces. Kathy Archer skillfully weaves together the personal and systemic aspects of leadership in a manner that is nuanced and personal."

TAMU THOMAS, transformational coach; author,
Women Who Work Too Much

"Kathy Archer has articulated the struggle of many women leaders and offers an illuminating model and actionable tactics to be the leader you were meant to be. A powerful and practical read for any leader struggling to lead with heart while also achieving success."

MARIA ROSS, author, *The Empathy Dilemma*;
host, *The Empathy Edge* podcast

"With a clear focus on the transformative power of character, Kathy Archer expertly blends intentional self-reflection with actionable guidance to help readers craft a leadership style that is authentic, ethical, and values driven. Through a well-thought-out five-step process, Kathy encourages leaders to examine their current character, define their aspirational identity, and develop a Character Development Plan that brings those principles to life in practice."

ELIZABETH BISHOP, founder, Elizabeth Bishop Consulting;
author, *Conscious Service*

"Diving into *Character Driven Leadership for Women* was like stepping into a masterclass tailored for women leaders in the nonprofit world. So often I feel a distinct weight of being a woman, of being my own worst enemy in trying to do too much, be everything to everyone, and pretending that I will prioritize my own self-care. Kathy Archer's focus on values over perfection and her practical tools for self-reflection left me feeling empowered to lead authentically. For anyone feeling the imposter syndrome's shadow (let me stand up) or striving to transform a network into a community, this book is comfort food with a dose of strategy."

TASHA VAN VLACK, CEO and co-founder, The Nonprofit Hive

"Kathy Archer brilliantly captures the essence of values-driven leadership, embracing both imperfection and the necessity of continuous learning. This book is more than just a read—it's a supportive tool to revisit time and again as we, women leaders, navigate the challenges and opportunities of developing values-aligned leadership."

HEATHER NELSON, CEO, BridgeRaise

"Every woman who is or aspires to be a leader needs this book. Insightful and immediately applicable, Kathy Archer's approaches will become your superpower to becoming more impactful and fulfilled in your career. Never have I read such a wealth of actionable knowledge packed into a few hundred pages."

ELIZABETH HORLOCK, Director of People and Culture, College of Nurses of Ontario

"This book is meant to cause a ripple in your thinking and behaviour, propelling you on your journey towards becoming your best self as a leader. You will go back to it, re-read it, highlight it, and use it as a resource again and again."

TANIA LITTLE CFRE, CSR-P, GCB.D, nonprofit leader

"This easy-to-read book provides women leaders with practical information and tools to guide their process. A must-read for all women in leadership."

LAVONNE ROLOFF, recipient of the Queen Elizabeth II's Platinum Jubilee medal

"This book comes at a time when doing more with less has become the mantra of the nonprofit sector. Leaders are driven to make decisions promptly and move onto the next decision quickly, so Kathy's advice to pause, ponder, pivot, and then proceed is counterintuitive. Yet, with less time to make decisions and act on them, it is critical to get the decision right the first time. Kathy's five steps help you to get the decision right the first time, building your credibility."

BILL SCOTT, Chief People Valuer, Valuing People

"Kathy Archer has done it again! *Character Driven Leadership for Women* is filled with useful frameworks and practical tools. Working through the book will support you on your journey to becoming the woman and leader that you aspire to embody."

NATALIE MCCARTHY, Executive Director, Association des entrepreneurs en maçonnerie du Québec

"Reading *Character Driven Leadership for Women* felt like having Kathy Archer by my side, guiding me through the highs and lows of nonprofit leadership. The book echoes many conversations from our coaching sessions. I appreciated the focus on health throughout the book; the emphasis on health, hope, and positivity truly stood out. I'll be keeping it close as my go-to guide."

PAM MCGLADDERY, President and CEO, Universal Rehabilitation Service Agency

"This book felt like a recap of all the conversations I've had with Kathy Archer in our coaching sessions. Reading the book will help a little, but *doing* even a fraction of what you read will help *a lot*. *Character Driven Leadership for Women* essentially contains the instructions for creating your own lifelong curriculum on how to be a better leader, and a better human being. And it's the next best thing to having Kathy on speed dial!"

SUE COUESLAN, VP, Strategy and Partnerships, Natural Products Canada

"*Character Driven Leadership for Women* is thought-provoking and inspiring! Kathy Archer nudges you towards finding your purpose and growing into your authentic self. She uses a great blend of leadership tools, self-guided exercises, and her own personal leadership experiences."

MEAGAN MAERZLUFT, PMO Manager, Enterprise Onboarding

"Kathy Archer is an amazing coach who is truly invested in supporting you in reaching your full potential as a leader. Her book is a roadmap for anyone wanting to look within and lead from a place of authenticity."

SHEENA MCKINNEY, Hub Manager, Mackenzie Family Resource Network

"In *Character Driven Leadership for Women*, Kathy Archer takes you on a journey. There may be a few bumps along this path of self-reflection, discovery, and character-building, but as Kathy notes, 'Leadership is a way of being.'"

LISA MACDONALD, Editor, *Hilborn Charity eNews*

Also by Kathy Archer

Mastering Confidence: Discover Your Leadership
Potential by Awakening Your Inner Guidance System

**Character
Driven
Leadership
for Women**

A 5-Step Guide to Shape Your Own Nonprofit Management Style with Strong Values, Ethics, and Morals

KATHY ARCHER

CHARACTER DRIVEN LEADERSHIP

FOR WOMEN

PAGE TWO

Cataloguing in publication information
is available from Library and Archives Canada.
ISBN 978-1-77458-548-1 (paperback)
ISBN 978-1-77458-549-8 (ebook)

Page Two
pagetwo.com

Edited by Emily Schultz
Copyedited by Crissy Boylan
Cover, interior design, and illustrations by Fiona Lee

kathyarcher.com

To my clients and students.
Your transformative leadership journey
is a testament to character driven
leadership and inspired these pages.

Contents

Part 4 **Making It Stick**

Why You Picked Up This Book

AS A WOMAN leading in a nonprofit, you might be faced with any of these situations:

- What others think about you isn't what you want them to think about you. Perhaps your reputation is sliding.

- You feel inauthentic, you feel like an impostor, and you've lost that sense of yourself.

- Burnout is looming. You've lost balance in your life, and you're sitting in survival mode, which doesn't feel good.

Overall, you'd like to be in a different place.

You'd like to enjoy impactful leadership. You want to make a difference, and you want to feel good doing it. That's enjoying impactful leadership.

Let's examine the flip side of those three points above.

- You want to feel respected, trusted, and engaged with your team and have a strong reputation.

- You want to feel more authentic, more like yourself, and comfortable in your own skin.

- You'd like to be thriving. Yes, you know there will be difficult days, and you won't always be in that utopian state. In fact, you may rarely get there, but when you start to slip, you would like to be able to regain your balance much more quickly.

That's what character driven leadership is.

Character driven leadership means acting on your morals, making value-based decisions, and following your own code of ethics, even when it's not easy. When you lead that way, you feel authentic and balanced.

The trap of pleasing, performing, or perfecting holds us back from leading with our strength of character.

- **Pleasing:** We tend to prioritize the needs and expectations of others over our own needs and desires. We want to be liked and accepted, even if it means sacrificing our own values or boundaries.

- **Performing:** As overachievers with high expectations, we feel a constant need to prove ourselves, to put on a facade of competence and capability even when feeling overwhelmed or uncertain.

- **Perfecting:** In our relentless pursuit of flawlessness, we believe every task, every project, and every decision must be perfect. This can lead to analysis paralysis, procrastination, and a fear of taking risks or making mistakes.

This pleasing, performing, and perfecting mentality leads us to burn out, feel like imposters, and sense a lack of authenticity in our leadership styles.

Character driven leadership requires you to lead with your authentic traits and use them optimally. It also means identifying which traits you want to grow, mature, or develop in yourself and continuing to do that for the rest of your life.

The key to intentional character development is intentional self-reflection. If you want to enjoy impactful leadership; feel respected, trusted, and engaged with your team; and feel authentic and thrive, then you must develop a habit of intentional self-reflection.

To be a character driven leader, you need to regularly reflect on the following questions:

- Who am I? (Character and reputation)
- Who am I becoming? (Aspirational identity)
- What am I doing to get there? (Growth)

To help you continually engage in self-reflection and review those character building questions, you'll learn a five-step model in this book called the Infinite Leadership Loop: pause, ponder, pivot, proceed, people. Yes, those five Ps are to help you remember the steps, but they're also tried-and-true techniques. The model was introduced in my first book, *Mastering Confidence*, which has helped thousands of women both develop confidence and feel more authentic. Finally, to keep you on track, you'll discover a series of practices to adopt to become the character driven leader you aspire to be.

But why is intentional self-reflection key to character development? Self-reflective practices are critically important because they help you make decisions. Engaging in self-reflection allows you to slow down and recognize your choice points, or opportunities to make decisions, and then make choices in a way that feels more aligned with who you are and who you are becoming. It is in those moments of intentional decision-making that you develop your character.

There are two parts you'll need to focus on: your character and your aspirational identity. Who you are is your character, and who you are becoming is your aspirational identity. Your character is who you are on your worst days, and your aspirational identity is who you are on your best days. This book aims to narrow the gap between those two.

Another way of thinking about it is that your character or reputation is how people describe you. It is the standards or filters where the expectations, beliefs, values, and morals that you are most committed to reside. Identity is who you are and what you aspire to be.

I may desire to be an honest person, but that doesn't mean I'm always honest. People may describe me (my character or my reputation) as choosing to be honest when it suits my needs. Once again, decisions are crucial for character building, but we aren't going to make conscious and intentional decisions without self-reflection.

That is why intentional self-reflection is so important to becoming a character driven leader. Self-reflection means intentionally choosing to slow down, pausing, and then pondering so you make the best decision, which is aligned with your aspirational identity. You will make more conscious choices once you've pivoted your perspective.

Then we unpause and return to action, with our people. Later, we will pause, reflect, and choose again in a continuous cycle of growth and development through self-reflection. Decisions build our character, and we make our best character driven decisions by pausing and pondering. Intentional self-reflection is key to character development.

Follow the steps in this book and you will get on the right track—the track that honours who you are and the work you are here to do, aligns with your values, and feels so much better! We will reconnect you with your authentic self. She is the self underneath all the layers that have been put on you over the years. We will unpack the judgments of others and, more importantly, the judgments you have of yourself.

I promise that by the end of this book you will have the tools you need to create your Character Development Plan and to implement it with success. Before we get there, let's start with where you might be at.

PART ONE

WHY ARE YOU STRUGGLING WITH YOUR LEADERSHIP STYLE?

Why You Hate Leadership

F YOU'VE PICKED UP this book, you're probably experiencing turmoil. Something has blown up in your outer world of leadership or life, or your inner world is unsettled. Perhaps both! Things are going wrong, sideways, or just plain bad. You're not happy, and it's time to change things.

Perhaps your work-life balance is shot, you're experiencing conflict with staff, or you're so overwhelmed that you don't even know what to do and have had enough. Maybe it's so bad that your team is unhappy with you. Whatever it is, you are unhappy with the you who is dealing with everything. It doesn't feel right. Maybe you are not proud of how you have handled certain things lately or of the person you've become. I understand—I've been there.

If we don't consciously deal with what is happening, we continue to react unconsciously. Like in the Whac-A-Mole game, we smack down whatever pops up, throw solutions at a continual bombardment of problems, and get caught up in the crisis of the day. With our hasty reactions to each "mole," we don't slow down to purposefully think about how we're dealing with things or the type of person we're being as we deal with them.

What's more, people notice.

You are at risk of becoming out of integrity when you are seen as frazzled, short, or unhinged. Despite making promises, we won't be able to deliver because we have too much on our plate or we aren't effectively prioritizing what we are responsible for. We tend to be short, bitter, or on edge, which adversely affects others. As a result, they might feel less comfortable approaching us. Instead, they might start gossiping about our poor responsiveness, mood, and lack of integrity.

Here's the thing: without realizing it, the ways people see us and talk about us have the potential to damage our character and our career. It did mine. I hit two big leadership lows that you'll hear about in the book.

You'll hear about the first leadership low later, but let me start with the second big leadership low that hit me in about 2009 when I was in a senior leadership position. I'd been managing everything on my plate and doing it with a level of confidence until the arrival of a large new contract. Increased responsibility, travel, staffing, scope, and budget all left me scrambling to hold things together. I felt as if I was in that old episode of *I Love Lucy* with the conveyor belt speeding faster and faster.

Because of that,

- I didn't always keep my word.

- I didn't follow through on promises.

- I neglected to listen to people's ideas and input. Instead, I railroaded through with my plan.

While my team had trusted me in the past, things changed dramatically. That year's feedback on my performance appraisal clearly indicated what the staff thought of me. I lacked integrity. It literally said, "Kathy lacks integrity!" Ooof!

I was frustrated, hurt, and discouraged by the feedback. Previous performance appraisals indicated I had strong trust with the team. How could things have plummeted so fast?

Without trust, my team was falling apart! When my team lost trust in me and felt I was out of integrity, they didn't feel they had a strong leader. As trust eroded, I lost followers in important ways:

- They didn't get behind my ideas.

- Their work performance dropped.

- They lacked enthusiasm when I delegated tasks to them.

There was no engagement, and the team cohesiveness was quickly eroding. In its place were tension, bickering, and whispering that stopped when I walked into the room. The decline culminated in a grievance filed against me. I was left fearful of being fired and, at the same time, ready to quit.

I was in survival mode, and it wasn't fun. Maybe you've felt like that before too. Perhaps you catch yourself saying things like "Just get me through today, please!" or "Just get me through this meeting/project/ trip!" These phrases are red flags indicating you might be stuck in survival mode, and you're merely trying to hang on rather than thrive.

As a nonprofit leader, you're no stranger to the constant ebb and flow of projects, budget cycles, and performance reviews. While this is part of the job, it's essential to recognize when you're slipping into survival mode. It's about not only the work itself but also your attitude toward it, how you manage your workload, and how it affects your overall well-being and relationships. Recognizing and addressing these challenges are integral to your leadership development journey.

But how did we end up where we are, feeling lost and out of sync with ourselves, in the first place? There is a good chance you moved into leadership without knowing what you were really getting into. You probably did frontline work and advanced because you were good at what you did. But did anyone ever teach you how to lead? Maybe not, so as you tried to navigate the leadership role, you figured there must be a right way to lead. Trying to emulate those leaders above you, you gradually became less and less authentically you and increasingly began to feel like an imposter.

I'm sorry you had to go through that. It's not fair. My goal is to change that for future generations of women leaders.

Let me introduce you to the surviving to thriving continuum. Recognizing your current position on this continuum is the first step in making intentional choices to move toward your desired position. Awareness is always the first step for positive change.

By acknowledging the range of positions you might occupy and the factors influencing your position, you can empower yourself to make intentional decisions that align with your goals and aspirations. This will ultimately foster a sense of fulfillment and purpose in your role as a nonprofit leader and help you lead with strong character, integrity, and authenticity.

Because You Are Stuck in Survival Mode

Are you stuck in survival mode? To help you assess where you are today, let's look at the three points on the surviving to thriving continuum.

Surviving

Survival mode is characterized by fear and negativity. You feel like you're constantly battling to keep things together, and your energy levels are low. You might feel isolated and unsupported, as if everyone is against you. In this state, burnout is a real risk. You are constantly on edge, trying to keep your head above water.

This is where I was when things fell apart with my team. I was barely hanging on!

Thriving

On the other end of the spectrum is thriving mode, where passion drives your actions. You're engaged, confident, and resilient, tackling challenges with ease. You feel supported and connected, making a positive impact through your work. Thriving is where the magic happens. It's about tapping into your energy, enthusiasm, and purpose to create a meaningful impact on your organization.

I'd been here in the past. It's what helped our team get the large contract.

Coping

Most of us, however, find ourselves somewhere in between, in what I call coping mode. Here, you're doing more than just surviving, but you're not fully thriving. It's a state of maintenance where you have good, so-so, and a few chaotic days. You might feel emotionally flat-lined, lacking excitement or joy.

When I was here, I didn't recognize the warning signs of impending survival mode.

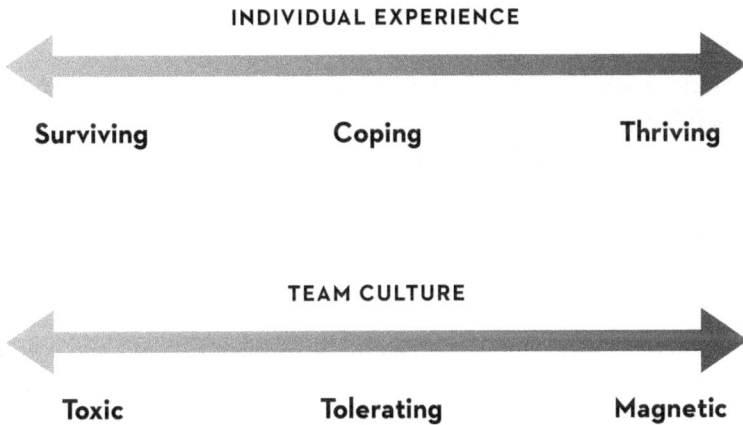

INDIVIDUAL EXPERIENCE

Surviving   **Coping**   **Thriving**

TEAM CULTURE

Toxic   **Tolerating**   **Magnetic**

The Intertwined Continuums

The surviving to thriving continuum is an individual experience that is closely intertwined with another continuum—the toxic to magnetic continuum—which pertains to organizational culture and team dynamics. My colleague Bill Scott and I developed this framework to aid leaders in comprehending diverse workplace cultures.

As leaders move along the surviving to thriving continuum, their mindsets, behaviours, and attitudes profoundly influence the workplace environment. When leaders operate in survival mode, characterized by fear, negativity, and burnout, it can foster a toxic atmosphere within the team. Conversely, thriving leaders radiate energy, passion, and resilience, creating a magnetic workplace culture where employees feel engaged, valued, and inspired.

The Toxic to Magnetic Continuum

Every workplace has its own unique culture—a vibe that influences how people feel and interact within the organization. From toxic environments that drain the life out of you to magnetic workplaces that inspire and energize, where does your organization fall on the spectrum?

Let's explore the characteristics of each point on the continuum. It might be toxic, tolerable, or magnetic.

Toxic

A toxic workplace is the energy vampire of workplace cultures. It is full of distrust, negativity, and high turnover. In a toxic work environment, individuals feel drained and demoralized, and team connections are strained. As I slipped into survival mode, my team quickly began demonstrating the behaviour of a toxic team.

Tolerable

The tolerable workplace is in the middle of the spectrum. You'll find varying degrees of toleration in the points along the centre. Here, it's not terrible enough to make you want to leave, but it's certainly not where you want to give your best effort. People tolerate the status quo, but deep down, they know there's room for improvement.

Magnetic

Now, the magnetic. Imagine a workplace where people feel an irresistible pull to be there because of the positive energy and sense of belonging. That's the essence of a magnetic workplace—a place where growth, openness, and creativity flourish and people are actively engaged in their work. It is the dream workplace.

Because You Play a Role in Workplace Culture

How much impact does a leader have on where the team is on the toxic-to-magnetic continuum? Perhaps more than you think. Gallup research has found that managers account for 70 percent of the variance in employee engagement. It's often said that people work for a boss, not an organization. You in your role as a leader impact your team more than the organization for which you work. This research underlines the importance of personal development and self-awareness, as your individual journey directly influences the culture and dynamics of your team.

Leaders serve as role models whose actions set the tone for the entire organization. How leaders navigate challenges, communicate with team members, and prioritize well-being send powerful signals about the organization's values and priorities.

In the nonprofit sector, where values and integrity are paramount, leaders must embody strength-based leadership and prioritize value-based decision-making. Women leaders can especially leverage their unique perspectives and strengths to foster inclusive and empowering environments within their organizations.

Leaders remain in survival mode when they neglect their own growth and self-care and rarely engage in purposeful work. This constant state of survival can influence the workplace environment, perpetuating a culture of stress, disengagement, and distrust among team members. This is where you may be headed if you don't do the self-reflective work in this book.

Conversely, leaders who prioritize personal growth, maintain a positive outlook, and foster a supportive environment contribute to a magnetic workplace culture that attracts and retains good workers committed to the organization, their own growth and development, and a work-life balance.

After my second big leadership low, I began to do my inner work by working with a coach. He helped me embrace my essence, who I was at my core. He helped me ponder my potential and the type of leader I could become. He also helped me see that leadership was

Leaders serve as role models whose actions set the tone for the entire organization.

a process of engaging in endless growth, most often about myself. I learned that self-reflection is the key to character development.

You, too, are on that journey if you choose to be. To become a character driven leader, you must repeatedly go through the same three self-reflective stages of learning:

1   **Embrace your essence:** Who am I?

2   **Ponder your potential:** Who am I becoming?

3   **Engage in endless growth:** How am I becoming that?

This journey will help you transition from surviving to thriving and in turn transform your team from toxic to magnetic. The work of character development involves increasing your awareness of where you land on the continuum at any given moment, identifying if a move is needed, and then doing what you need to do to get where you want to be. As a nonprofit leader seeking to develop yourself and create a more engaged team and robust workplace culture, you need a model for this self-reflective work. Here's a quick introduction to the model.

Because You Need the Infinite Leadership Loop

The model you'll learn in this book is the Infinite Leadership Loop (which you can find on page 120). The Infinite Leadership Loop, an advanced iteration of a model pioneered by Bill Scott and myself, illustrates the ongoing dance between self-reflection and action, which is vital for effective leadership. Curiosity fuels this continuous back and forth, driving progress even amid hesitations, doubts, and the reluctance to be vulnerable.

On the left side of the loop is a process of accessing your inner wisdom through the Inner Guidance System. By doing this, leaders engage in self-reflection and introspection to gain clarity on their values, strengths, and areas for improvement. By pausing, pondering, pivoting, and proceeding, leaders cultivate a deeper understanding of themselves and their leadership approach, allowing them to make intentional decisions that align with their vision for personal and organizational success.

The right side of the Infinite Leadership Loop encourages leaders to engage with their teams and foster meaningful connections through active listening, collaboration, correction, and empowerment.

Moving through the points of the Infinite Leadership Loop— pause, ponder, pivot, proceed, and people—you'll be navigating your own personal growth journey while simultaneously shaping a vibrant and supportive workplace culture. You'll create a workplace where people feel valued, engaged, and excited to make a difference. You'll unleash your organization's full potential and create a workplace where people thrive.

Leading authentically, thriving, and creating a magnetic workplace sounds wonderful, but you may not be there. Right now, you may feel like you don't even know who you are. If so, read on.

And Because You've Lost Sight of Your Identity

Have you lost sense of who you really are? I certainly had. Most of us have spent the last five, ten, or twenty-five years focusing on just getting through the day or the week. What's more, we've spent the last five, ten, or twenty-five years trying to hide, cover up, or change who we are at our core.

We have been embarrassed or ashamed about who we are, so we've tried to hide the parts of ourselves that don't seem to fit into the world as we know it. We were taught, often subconsciously, by the work world that we should lead with a more masculine leadership style—directive, task-oriented, hierarchical, and competitive—and that we should leave our emotional, creative, and relationship-oriented traits at the door. What are typically considered feminine traits have not been valued as professional or effective; therefore, we have not valued those qualities in ourselves.

In reality, women possess characteristics that make them adept managers, impactful leaders, and catalysts for transformation—

often surpassing men in these roles. One of our common key strengths is our ability to foster team engagement, which results in significant business success.

So, how do you find and embrace those things about yourself that you've covered up, pushed down, or tried to eradicate? Partly, that is the work of this book. It's about creating your future identity with intention.

Your identity is how you define yourself, the story you tell about who you are, and the lens through which you see yourself now and in the future.

So often, we feel uncomfortable, awkward, and ashamed, and we know we are not being our authentic and best selves. It's frustrating and often humiliating. We don't realize that we don't know who we are anymore. We know we feel crappy, but it's hard to place our finger on what's wrong. We blame our workload, another person, or society. But to be any more specific than that, it is often a bit harder. In truth, we've become so unaligned that we've lost sight of who we are. And we act out of character, or like the character we desire to be seen as. Like I had been, you may want to be a leader who leads with integrity but are not truthfully walking your talk.

If you are like so many women I work with, you might think, "I don't even know who I am anymore!" You feel a constant inner turmoil nagging at you. It happens to many women. They feel that inner turmoil physically in their body.

- The tension headache begins when they stay late at work again and miss their daughter's dance recital.

- The anxiety bubbles as they walk into the staff meeting. They don't want to share a tough decision, especially one they morally disagree with.

- The knot tightens in their stomach when they feel forced to let someone go even though they know it's wrong to do so.

- Their heart pounds when they communicate to the funder but omit certain points they were told not to share. They know they are being misleading, even dishonest, but what can they do?

That inner turmoil is felt because they've lost connection with who they are. The inner turmoil is warning them that their actions and behaviours are out of sync with who they want to be. For some, the chasm has become so wide between the two lines that they can no longer see across—they can't see their authentic self anymore. They don't know who they are. They just know this isn't it. They aren't clear about who they want to be, but they know their day-to-day reality doesn't match their inner desires. They feel incongruent. What's more, they don't feel they can control who they are.

The tug inside is that small voice we keep trying to quiet, as it whispers that something is not right.

We often connect our sense of self-worth to what we do and our titles, as if our titles give us credibility. However, we are walking a slippery slope when we define ourselves by what we do. It leaves us unable to be without the job or the title. We feel lost, unattached to anything, and unanchored. Some of us feel exposed, vulnerable, or unworthy. We must perform well or else we feel we aren't worthy. This is the perfect breeding ground for perfectionism.

I felt lost when I left the company I'd worked for after the better part of twenty years. I didn't have the title, the role, the activities, the community, or the friends to define who I was, what I did, and the impact I had. It was just Kathy. Not program director or manager or chairperson or committee member or someone's boss. Just Kathy. It left me feeling both naked and disoriented. I had no title to define who I was and no daily role to act out. It's taken me years to find my way without the roles or titles. The self-reflective work I've done has helped me find my way.

When you are lost, you have lost sight of your self-identity. Your self-identity is what makes you, you. Take a moment to consider:

- How are you unique?

- How are you any different than any other woman leader?

- What makes you stand out from others in your hierarchy, organization, or sector?

It's hard work to keep up pretenses, to live a lie. It is draining to wear a disguise. Carrying the armour, cloak, guard, or shield all day—that's heavy! This drains you of the energy and resources you need to do the real work of leading. And it leaves you not feeling like yourself.

The problem is that you've done it for so long that you don't know how many layers you have on, and you have forgotten what is under them.

You are afraid someone will discover "the real you" underneath and judge you for not being a worthy or capable leader, so you don't let your guard down. But that is exactly what I want you to do. Character comes from your individual traits, and those traits are your pathways to leading authentically. I want you to uncover who you are, gently, slowly, and in a nonjudgmental way.

I want you to discover that underneath your disguise that you armour up with every day—to be "professional," "right," and "proper"—is a person who is

- beautiful
- talented
- gifted
- genuine
- powerful
- smart
- capable
- joyous
- authentically you

In this book, you will learn how to uncover, redefine, or create your new aspirational identity. You'll take parts of yourself you want to keep, grow them, and mature them. You will let go of parts that aren't serving you and choose new ones to plant, nurture, and develop—all while developing your leadership character.

Underneath the layers of shoulds, musts, and have-tos, your soul is crying out for you to realign with the real, genuine, bona fide you underneath. To do that, you must engage in intentional self-reflection to help you realign.

Finding Alignment

Imagine two lines. One line is your values, beliefs, personality, and ethics—your measuring stick or gauge. The other line is your behaviours, decisions, actions, and morals. You feel good when your behaviours and actions are in alignment with your beliefs and values. The further you stray from that measuring stick, the worse you feel. That's what it feels like to be aligned or unaligned.

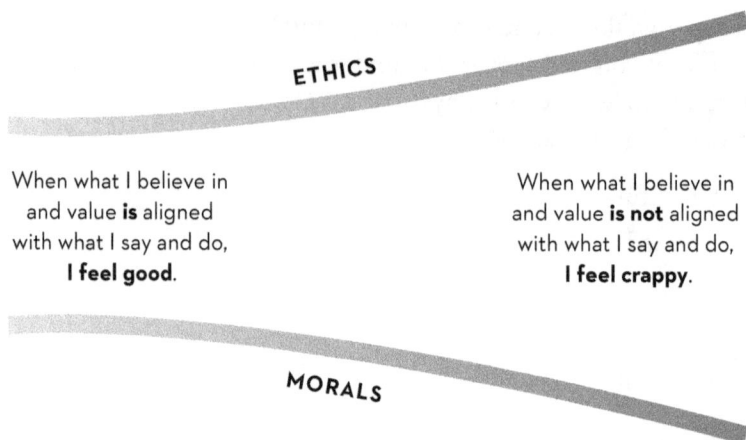

ETHICS

When what I believe in
and value **is** aligned
with what I say and do,
I feel good.

When what I believe in
and value **is not** aligned
with what I say and do,
I feel crappy.

MORALS

When you are aligned, you are living in integrity. Integrity is when your actions are in harmony with your values, beliefs, morals, and ethics. If you do something that isn't aligned, you feel crappy, and you compromise your integrity and your reputation—which take a split second to destroy and years to build up. Therefore, we need to make wise decisions that are aligned with the person (and the leader) we really want to be!

We are continually moving toward or away from alignment. Every thought, decision, and action move you further away from or closer to that guiding line. Here are some examples.

- If you value family time but neglect your family for weeks, you feel crappy. You've moved away from your values.

- When you disconnect from work for a weekend and focus on your kids, mother, or partner, you step back into alignment.

- When you've been busy and stressed, you may feel physically drained. On top of that, if you value health and well-being, you may be disappointed or frustrated that you're not taking care of yourself. You've moved away from your measuring stick, causing you to feel unaligned.

- If you take time off to rest, you're acting in harmony with your values of health and well-being, and you feel better. As a result, you also feel more balanced and back in alignment.

So many of us stray too far from our measuring stick and always feel off. What's worse, we spend more time unaligned than aligned. We deviate further from what we believe to be important, what we care for, and what we stand for. We lose clarity on our values and how we define them. Our perception gets cloudy. We blur lines, stretch truths, and cover up indiscretions.

While we were once adamant we'd never be away from home for more than one night, suddenly it's become a week-long work trip. Then a couple of trips a month. We may justify our decision to prioritize work over our family or relationships: "They know I care about them! They are okay with me doing this for a few days or weeks." But have those days and weeks become months? They did for me sadly.

And then there are the issues at work as you become unaligned. If you are short with your team once, that's being human. But when you snap more often than you are measured or calm, it's become the norm. When your standard response is short and terse, your team won't trust you when you are patient because you rarely are anymore. They know it's only a matter of time before you are jumping down their throats again with demands.

Do you remember Maslow's hierarchy of needs? He suggested that we move up the pyramid from safety and security to self-actualization. However, we can also move down instead of up: "In any given moment, we have two options: to step forward into growth or to step back into safety." When we veer too far from that measuring stick of who we are and what we believe in, our self-esteem drops, we lose connection to those we love, our world becomes unsafe, and our basic needs are not being met. In truth, we are in survival mode.

You cannot lead with your strength of character when you are at the bottom of the pyramid. You need to take one step forward into growth rather than slipping back down the side of the pyramid! Even if that one step is only a tiny move up. This book shows you how.

2

What Does Character Have to Do with It?

'VE TOUCHED ON character many times already, but what is it, and what does it really mean for leadership?

Leadership isn't a thing you do, your title, or your role. It's a way of being. Leadership is your unique expression of who you are—in essence, your character. That is why no two leaders are the same and why we like or love some leaders more than others.

A leader's job is to influence others so together you do the mission critical work. Leaders set the direction. Your character and conduct influence your employees. How you conduct yourself impacts their actions, responses, and reactions; their choices, attitudes, and mindsets. You are role modelling for them.

Leading is about motivating, inspiring, coaching, and mentoring others. The effectiveness of all of that comes down to how we do it. It is the manner in which we motivate, inspire, coach, and mentor that both develops our character and our relationships with employees. It is based on how we conduct ourselves.

Consider respect:

- Do your employees respect you?
- Does your character demand their respect?
- Are you the type of person they would respect?

Our character—or perhaps more aptly put our *lack* of character—is the biggest reason for leadership failure. Leaders without integrity fail to gain the trust of their team. Leaders who have no courage fail to rally those around them to do the risky work. Leaders without the ability to exercise self-control fly off the handle, fall apart emotionally, or make snap judgments. Leaders who have little hope and optimism create a doom-and-gloom environment, which isn't much fun to work in.

The problem is many of us ask what we have to do to be a better leader: "What training do I need to take? What actions do I need to do?" While those are important components of leadership, the critical question is deeper than that. It's not what you have to *do* to be a good leader; the question is *who* you need to *be*.

Consider the *how* of what you do:

- Anyone can run a meeting. But *how* do you run a meeting?

- CEOs, executive directors, and managers communicate with their teams all the time. But *how* do you communicate with your team?

- Who are you *being* when you address an employee's poor performance or share positive outcomes with the team?

- Who are you *being* when the crisis hits?

How People Describe You

Who are you being when you do your job is a description of your character. It's the essence of who you are. Consider how we describe other people and how others might describe you. Pay attention to the word "character" in each sentence.

- Often, we talk about someone's character in general statements such as "I admire her character."

- We might say someone has sound character.

- In a tongue-in-cheek tone, we might chuckle, saying, "Boy, she's quite the character!"

- We might whisper to a friend that something was out of character for her.

- We might groan as we watch someone do something and say, "She just damaged her character by doing that!"

Now, think about specific descriptions of other people's character traits. Consider, again, how people might describe your traits. These are some ways we speak in awe of certain women's characteristics:

- She is so reliable.

- I love her honesty.

- What grace she has!

- That is a woman of integrity.

- She has such determination and persistence.

- I appreciate her ability to be decisive.

- She has a clear head on her shoulders.

Don't forget that not all character traits are perceived as good. Reflect on this list below. We cringe at character traits that some women display:

- She's so cold.

- I can't trust her.

- She's condescending and demeaning.

Your character is your unique combination of qualities, values, and traits that distinguish you from others and that make you, you. It is how others perceive you; it's not how you see yourself or how you wish others would see you. You certainly can impact or influence what others think about you, and you should. Ultimately, how people describe your character is their perception, which makes character development tricky.

Leading with Strong Character

Why do we struggle to lead with our strong character traits? First, because we've never really taken the time to get to know ourselves. Second, because what we see in ourselves, we don't always like or think is helpful, useful, or right, so we push it away, looking to find a better way. Third, because we tend to avoid inner work, reflective processes, and anything that might take us out of our comfort zone. And remember, self-reflection is key to character development.

The word "character" comes from the Greek word "kharaktēr," which originally referred to a stamping tool or instrument used for engraving or marking. It's the marking or distinctive quality that gives something its character.

In the same way, we develop our character by chiselling our unique marks. Character isn't developed by "finding yourself." Instead, it starts with uncovering yourself. What are the unique qualities and traits at your core that make you, you? The work of character development matures those qualities. Clients will often say to me, "I'm honest. I can't help it. I just say things that are true." But they also admit that quality gets them into trouble sometimes. Just as you wouldn't give a four-year-old the same explanation about where babies come from as you would a fourteen-year-old, we can learn to manage our characteristics by turning them up or down depending on situations. The key to character development is being in control of the dial and being aware of when to adjust it.

The second part of character development is adding or removing the traits that help shape us into a person we are proud of, love, and accept. Think of how your signature has changed over the years. It's still your signature, just a more refined and mature version of your signature.

Character development begins with becoming aware of your values, ethics, morals, skills, talents, and traits and learning to live in alignment with them. That way you will feel matched with who you are and no longer "out of character."

Then it is about looking at the impact you want to have on others and the difference you want to make in the world. That vision allows you to determine which parts of your current character will help you do that. It also identifies new or different character traits, values, ethics, and morals that you must strengthen, grow, or develop.

Perhaps you're wondering if character development is about getting people to like you. No, that's not quite it. Your job as a leader is to guide people by inspiring them to grow and develop so that together you can reach your shared vision. Your influence can motivate people to be their best selves, which is incredibly helpful in reaching team and organizational goals and serving clients. Achieving that level of impact on others is certainly easier if they like you. Even so, it's less about people liking you and more about them respecting you.

To deepen your understanding of character, take a moment to fill in these blanks:

- My boss has a reputation for _____
- My board chair is known for _____
- You can always trust the head of HR to _____
- That employee is famous for _____

Perhaps these are some of the sentence endings you came up with:

- Flying off the handle at meetings
- Not letting people speak
- Interrupting
- Being patient
- Inspiring the team

- Being there when I need them
- Knowing exactly what I need to hear

Consider how people would describe you. If your answers are not how you want them to think of your character, it might be time to change that.

Your Conduct and Reputation

While your character is how others describe you and your impact on them, your conduct is the behaviours and actions that others use to assess your character. This includes how you act, interact, and engage with others. It is what you say and do as much as what you don't say or don't do.

- Are you late? Often?
- Do you swear? In public?
- Are you decisive or wishy-washy?
- How do you share hard messages?
- When something exciting happens, what can people expect from you?
- What's your default response when things don't go as planned?
- Do you walk into a meeting with checklists, agendas, and handouts ready to get down to business and with a smile on your face, or are you rushed, frazzled, and oblivious to everyone in the room?

Your answers to these questions will provide some insights into how others might describe your character. Each incident, response, or action doesn't stand alone. People use the sum of all your conduct to assess your character.

Another way to describe your character is also your reputation. It's what people say about you.

- She's so...
- She's known for...
- She's seen as...
- She can be counted on to...
- She can be trusted for...
- You can expect *X* from her...
- Don't expect *X* from her...

In essence, your character is how you make others feel: how they know you, how they describe you, and how they expect you to act.

Their description is based on your conduct. It is your actions or inactions that create feelings and then the labels that others give you. It is how you engage and disengage with others. And it results in what others say about you:

- Behind your back
- When they are gossiping or venting
- To their spouse or their work bestie

Leading people with intention in how you show up, conduct yourself, interact, and act is how you strengthen your character. Your character is more than a list of traits you aspire to; it is how you conduct yourself and thus live that list. It is about your morals and ethics, which are demonstrated through your actions. It starts with your intentions but ultimately, to influence others' assessments of your character, you must manage your conduct with intention.

Regardless of whether you're prepared or caught off guard, energized or exhausted, early or running behind, in control or taken by surprise—you always have the power to choose how you show up, and that choice defines your character.

People also judge the things you don't say or do. They may judge you negatively when you don't show up, disengage, pull back, or shut down. They may appreciate when you stay quiet and listen without getting defensive.

Yes, people are constantly judging and evaluating your conduct. By judging your conduct, they are formulating their opinions of your character. Remember, it's not only what you say but how you say it.

- How do you show up in stressful times?
- How do you deal with unexpected events?
- What is your automatic reaction when you don't have time to think?

As you develop your character, consider that not all of our behaviours are equal. Often the bad times outweigh the good ones. It takes a long time to forgive, let go, or heal. The question is if you do the work after, such as making an apology to repair a relationship. No one expects you to be perfect, but what do you do after you are less than perfect?

Our unconscious behaviour often carries more weight than our conscious decisions. This is why we will spend a lot of time later in the book looking at the habits we create.

Gestures, body language, and tone count more than words. Consider your nonverbal messages. Our bodies, especially our faces, give away more than we realize. This nonverbal communication plays a huge role in how others judge our character. Below are some examples of what others might say to their peers in response to conduct, based on our nonverbals.

- She just sits there with resting bitch face.
- Oh boy, I just got "the look."
- She was seething with anger.
- The sarcasm dripped out of her.
- Her face looked like it could crack.
- I could tell she wanted to cry.
- Her eyes were smiling.
- Her laughter was infectious.
- She wears her heart on her sleeve.
- I could feel her lean in; it felt like she really cared.

Leadership isn't
a thing you do, your
title, or your role.
It's a way of being.

Think about what these comments say about the employees' ideas of their leader's character.

I expect you are understanding more and more why your character is so important. When your character is strong, you have a good reputation. It's that reputation that garners others' respect. Let me say it again: someone doesn't have to like you to respect you. The two do not always go hand in hand. It's respect, though, that allows your team to be patient with you, persist for you, and push themselves. Respect for you, which is often because they believe in you and your message, is inextricably intertwined with your character. You will inspire and motivate your team with your actions, your conduct, and the type of person you are.

People define your character by your conduct. It's your interactions with them that impact what they think of you. But what they think about you is not the end point. Their opinion of you is only the catalyst for their behaviour. Your actions, your conduct, and in essence your character in any given moment influences others in one of two directions: backwards or forward. They will either take positive action or negative action.

If you've just been short with your team during a staff meeting, your actions, tone, and message may have left a bad taste in their mouths. Now they have a couple of options. First, they can head over to the water cooler and whisper about what time of the month it is for you. If that doesn't feel like a good idea, they might just head back to their office, keeping out of your way. Back in the safety of their offices, they'll procrastinate and check their newsfeeds. The chance that they will take proactive action to get the team back on track is slim to none. They may be motivated to bring you the late report or pull the reins a little tighter on their team, but consider the tone they will be doing it in. I doubt they'll be enthusiastic, eager, or engaging.

I'm not suggesting we need to be chipper all the time, but as you'll see, it's the sum of your actions and behaviours over time that determines how others define your character. How you conduct yourself in stressful times tends to outweigh people's memory of your conduct during smoother times. Therefore, we need to be even more diligent about our behaviour during difficult times.

Why Is Character Important in Leadership?

Why is character important in leadership? As you've seen now, character driven leaders create trust with their people and create an engaging work environment.

Because much of our behaviour is automatic, habitual, reactionary, or rote, we don't think about it; we are not conscious, and often our unchecked emotions are running the show. We may not be creating the impact we desire. For example:

- If we are mad, we snap.

- If we are annoyed, we are short with someone.

- If we run out of time, we don't bother to look up, acknowledge someone, or take a moment to see what's happening.

That kind of behaviour does not create strong followers or develop leadership in our employees. Instead, it creates a toxic work environment where people put up with things counting down the minutes until they can go home at the end of the day or find another job.

Watching Dr. Benjamin Hardy explain character development was revolutionary for me. I'm not going to lie: I've binge-watched his YouTube channel and read all of his books. I've described his ideas of how we create character to many clients who finally get it. Here's my rendition of Dr. Hardy on character development.

Our aspirational identity is our ceiling. It's the person we aim to be, our highest self, the best version of who we are. This is our target. But rarely are we there. Our character is our floor. This is us, I'll say, at our worst. It's what people actually experience. So, while I aim to be a responsive leader, in truth, sometimes I am, and sometimes I'm not. While my desire is to have work-life balance, I don't achieve that all the time.

The goal of character development is to reduce the gap between our floor and our ceiling. And to raise our floor. The floor is how low you will go. What's the worst you will let yourself be? Where's your line?

If you say you run staff meetings monthly but skip one month, maybe that's not the end of the world for you and your team. But two months? How about three? What if you haven't had a team meeting in six months? How low will you go? That bottom bar is how people will describe you. "Inconsistent," "disorganized," or "uncommitted" are the words that they might use.

We need to define our ceiling, the person we are aiming to be. We need an aspirational identity. That is much of the work in this book. Who do you want to become? What is the target you are aiming for? And how much effort are you willing to put in to get there? If you have some ideas now, jot them down as you continue to read.

You Never Finish Developing Your Character

Your character is not static: you don't get there, and you're done. It is something you'll need to focus on for the rest of your life.

When I moved into full-time leadership in about 1999, things got messy fast, and I hit my first big leadership low. As a new young leader, I hadn't had any specific leadership training. I moved up because I knew the job well and demonstrated leadership potential.

Knowing I didn't have the education or experience, I struggled with imposter syndrome. Things started to overwhelm me. I was now supervising my peers, which brought new challenges. The staff weren't happy with nonprofit wages and brought the union in. By Christmas that year, I was falling apart. Despite that, I tried hard to do my job, so I planned the staff holiday party—and only three people showed up. Depressed and not sure I ever wanted to go back to work, I took two weeks off and tried, albeit not very successfully, to "enjoy the holiday."

By January, I was sitting in my doctor's office sobbing and walked out with a prescription for antidepressants. It was one of the lowest points in my career. I didn't know if I wanted to return to work; I wasn't sure I was cut out for the job. But something in me wouldn't let it go.

Not only did I return to work, but I returned to school. It was then that I decided to begin my leadership education, taking one course at a time to attain my management degree. It took eight years. I did a lot of learning, experienced immense growth, and felt a personal transformation through self-discovery work.

To help with my growth, I created a curriculum for my personal and leadership development. I read books from authors like Cheryl Richardson and Wayne Dyer, learning to care for myself and balance life. I took self-tests like CliftonStrengths and VIA Character Strengths to identify my skills and talents and discern areas for growth. I took courses from the local college, our adult education society, and any training I could convince my organization to pay for. I bought books on team building, leadership, management, and networking with every spare dime I could find. By developing my curriculum, I was able to grow myself as a leader and as a person.

Honestly though, I didn't realize how much I was growing, but others did. In 2008, my boss wrote about how committed I was to improving myself:

> I have witnessed how she transformed herself as a person ... Kathy has worked as well on her inner self, and I can see this every time I talk with or see Kathy. Her confidence, inner security, and calmness shines out from inside her. Kathy radiates her inner assurance to others, and this is a quality that is quite remarkable. Kathy really has become a leader because of her inner strength, not because of her title.

That demonstration of inner strength and self-assurance didn't last. Less than two years later, I hit my second leadership low after we got a large contract, and my confidence and competence level didn't match the demands and expectations of the job. It was then that I fell out of integrity. What I then learned—and what we'll cover next—is how to get back into leading with integrity. A big part of that was learning to manage my emotions. Let's start there.

3

What Do Emotions Have to Do with It?

F AR TOO MANY women leaders believe that displaying emotions in the workplace is wrong. The traditional stoicism often associated with masculine leadership makes women feel the need to suppress their emotions to fit in. Consequently, women may struggle to find authentic ways to lead, as they navigate the disconnect between societal norms and their own natural inclinations. At the same time, men in leadership roles may inadvertently reinforce these expectations by role modelling emotional restraint.

Subconsciously, we've learned to set aside how we feel to get the job done.

- We put on fake smiles.

- We lie when people ask how we are feeling.

- We push down the rage, the sadness, and the fear.

- We armour up with a mask to prevent people from seeing what's happening inside.

You probably want to shut your emotions off just as many of my clients do. I tried to do that too. But it didn't work for me, and trust me, it won't work for you. You can't lead authentically without tuning in to how you feel. Do these statements sound familiar?

- I want to handle tough conversations without becoming angry, snapping, or getting defensive.

- I want to deal with challenging client situations that pull my heartstrings without crying.

- I want to stay focused and on top of things and bring calm to the team when stressors are building.

I've had all these feelings, and so have many of my clients and students. Try as I might to shut off, tune out, or compartmentalize my emotions, they more often than not bubble up to the surface at the most inopportune times or hijack me out of nowhere. I'd shut the door a little harder than necessary. I'd be terse with someone when I meant to be patient. When I so desperately needed a hug from my husband at the end of the day, I'd criticize him for something because I was afraid that if I got a hug, I'd start sobbing uncontrollably without being able to explain why.

If you've ever lost your composure at work (and we all have), you know how unsettling it can be! It can be embarrassing, and it sometimes feels hard to bounce back.

Back in 1999, I was suddenly supervising my peers after moving from a frontline position to a leadership position. Feeling unsure of myself and lacking the confidence to address issues calmly, I remember yelling at my administrative support one day. As soon as I did, I regretted it. I couldn't take back what I'd said. Not long after, she quit.

While we can't change the past, we can slow down what is happening inside us and positively impact what we say and how we behave, thus reducing the number of times we say or do something we regret. Shutting off emotions is impossible. When we try to tune them out, they negatively impact our leadership and character. As author and speaker Joan Borysenko reminds us, "Emotions are messages about the world, and repressing them simply keeps us in ignorance. It doesn't qualify us for sainthood."

Just because you experience an emotion, it does not mean you need to express that emotion in any particular way. The problem isn't that you *experience* emotions. The challenge lies in how you *express* your emotions.

To prevent your emotions from hijacking you, you must first learn to recognize them as you experience them and then manage how you express them. It's hard to do in the moment without first practising. You need to review situations after the fact. Self-reflection is key to leadership development. Looking back at an incident and dissecting what happened helps develop your emotional intelligence. This is self-reflection. This is the work of a leader.

Embracing emotions at work isn't wrong; it's about becoming an emotionally intelligent leader who decides when and how to express emotions. Leaders with emotional intelligence maintain stronger reputations by managing their emotional expression rather than suppressing it. Remember, you can control how you express your emotions rather than letting them control you.

Emotionally intelligent leaders don't lose it when someone says something that sparks their anger or annoyance. A leader in control of what's happening inside them will be aware they are irritated but can catch themselves before they roll their eyes, sigh, or let a sarcastic comment slip out.

To increase your emotional intelligence, you'll learn to use the Infinite Leadership Loop. Learning to respond consciously rather than react unconsciously builds your character. You want to get to the point where you pause before reacting. Consider and choose how you want to express an emotion before you act. This management of emotions is a key characteristic of an emotionally intelligent leader.

Composure is a self-controlled state of mind. This means you can think your way to being composed.

———————

What Is Emotional Intelligence?

You've probably heard about emotional intelligence. But you may wonder, "What is it? And how do you get it, do it, or be it?" Let's start with some definitions of terms used to discuss emotional intelligence and why they matter to you and your leadership.

When we talk about shutting our emotions off, what most of us really mean is that we want to be composed in conversations, meetings, and our day-to-day work. You are composed when you are calm and free from agitation.

"Composure," a noun, is something you can lose, keep, regain, or maintain. It's your ability to stay calm. If you lose your composure, you're freaking out or falling apart. When you stay calm under pressure, you're keeping your composure.

Staying calm under pressure is an almost daily requirement of leadership. We are constantly bombarded with expectations, rapid-fire communications from emails to chats, and multiple meetings in quick succession, all while dealing with staff shortages, being underfunded, and, as you know, in the nonprofit sector, this list goes on.

Composure is a self-controlled state of mind.

Read that last sentence again. Composure is a self-controlled state of mind. This means you can think your way to being composed.

Being self-controlled or having self-restraint is a result of *self-regulation.*

Self-regulation is managing what one feels and does and displaying appropriate control of impulses and emotions.

Can you see why self-regulation of emotions is important?

- I wanted to regulate my anger and not slam the door.

- I tried to control my impulse to be terse, but to do that, I needed to manage my irritation.

- I wanted to follow through on my impulse to ask my husband for a hug, but I didn't want the waterworks to be uncontrolled.

According to *Merriam-Webster*, "emotion" is "a conscious mental reaction (such as anger or fear) subjectively experienced as a strong feeling usually directed toward a specific object and typically accompanied by physiological and behavioural changes in the body."

Notice the words "mental reaction" in that definition. Once again, I want to highlight the thinking part of this definition. You can think your way into different emotions.

The challenge is that we want to shut off our emotions so that we don't get emotional, because women often get labelled emotional, and lord knows we don't want to be told we are being too emotional!

Being emotional is when we are dominated by showing or revealing strong emotions. When we are emotional, we often feel and are considered by others to be out of control of our emotions. That's not a very fun feeling! Unfortunately, it's also associated with weakness in the eyes of many.

So what's the answer? It's to become emotionally intelligent.

In *Becoming a Resonant Leader*, Annie McKee, Richard Boyatzis, and Frances Johnston describe emotional intelligence as "the ability to process emotional information quickly and accurately, to recognize one's own emotions as they happen, and to immediately understand their effects on oneself and others."

When we are emotionally intelligent, we tune in rather than shut off our emotions. We learn from the emotions we are experiencing. Just because we are experiencing a particular emotion doesn't mean we express it freely. Instead, we use self-regulation to consider how we express it, if at all.

When we are emotionally intelligent, we learn to distinguish emotions and clarify what we are feeling. So instead of the basic four emotions—happy, sad, mad, and glad—we use our emotional literacy to go deeper.

Getting Granular: Finely Tuned Feelings

As a leader, it's helpful to understand the difference between feeling uneasy about our staff's decision and being frightened about its results. One may have us bring it up in next week's conversation. The other might have us picking up the phone immediately. This ability to clearly label what we are feeling is called *emotional granularity*.

Psychologist Lisa Feldman Barrett tells us that emotional granularity is the skill of labelling experience with a high degree of specificity. If you have "finely tuned feelings," you're exhibiting emotional granularity. It's like taking salt crystals and grinding them down into smaller pieces. Are you feeling afraid or apprehensive? Distressed, fearful, or uptight? There is a difference between feeling scared or uneasy, nervous or hesitant. When you drill down and get specific, you gain more insight into what's happening and what may help you manage your emotions. To help you identify your emotions, use the Feelings Wheel (feelingswheel.com). This tool helps you visualize the range and intensity of emotions and provides some vocabulary so you get more specific in describing your feelings.

When you can clarify what you are feeling with precision and then express that during a tough conversation, meeting, or email, you are demonstrating emotional granularity. Instead of just feeling angry, you may notice you feel provoked, let down, or betrayed. This clarity helps to plan your response better.

Each of these terms works together. You must self-regulate your emotions to remain composed and keep your composure through stressful times. You'll develop your emotional intelligence as you use your expanding emotional vocabulary (or emotional literacy) to describe your feelings with increasing specificity—emotional granularity. You can see why self-reflection is so important to emotional intelligence and character development. As Dr. Daniel Siegel recommends, when you name your emotions, you tame them.

Your staff needs you to be composed. That doesn't mean you never feel angry, hopeless, or afraid. These are real emotions that you will feel at times, along with a zillion others. It's not the emotions that are wrong; it's how you deal with them. Anger, for instance, is unavoidable; however, you need to be mad at the right times and with the right people in the right way. Hopelessness will enter your space again and again. However, you can't hang on to it and spew it to those around you. Especially in a mission-driven organization, you need to notice that feeling of hopelessness and then move it along. It's not going to help you or the people who need you.

The question is *not* "How do I shut my emotions off?" The question is "How do I manage my intense emotions while still maintaining my composure?"

Instead of suppressing our emotions, we must learn to manage them. Managing your emotions, or emotional intelligence, is a cornerstone of effective leadership. By learning to manage your emotions effectively, you'll strengthen your composure, resilience, and ability to lead with empathy and authenticity. Now that you have a better understanding of why your emotions matter so much, let's talk about some other key aspects of leadership. Don't worry, you'll soon learn more about how to develop emotional intelligence as part of your Character Development Plan.

4

What They Never Taught You About Leadership

EADERSHIP IS A way of being: how you take action and communicate. Remember what I said earlier: it's not your title or your role. When you lead well, your personality, style, vision, method, and character influence your followers, swaying them toward a vision of a positive future.

As is typical in the nonprofit sector, you likely weren't trained in many areas as you transitioned into a leadership position—in not just what to do but how to do it. Perhaps no one explained the difference between managing people and leading people.

Leadership Is Different Than Management

We often use the words "managing" and "leading" interchangeably. However, these terms don't mean the same thing. The truth is you do both. Sometimes, you manage and lead at different times. On other occasions, you do both simultaneously. So why bother understanding the difference between management and leadership?

The answer is simple: you need to develop your skills in both areas. The challenge is that we get caught up in managing. We spend most of our time, heads down, just trying to survive, and we lose sight of leading.

To understand the difference, think of a boat: a manager steadies it to keep it from tipping, while a leader steers it forward. You need both roles to get anywhere. Managers seek stability, order, and consistency while maintaining the status quo. They minimize risks by managing budgets, setting up work schedules, and ensuring people fulfill their job descriptions. In essence, managers get the work done. Leaders move things forward by challenging the status quo. Leaders focus on change, movement, and growth by looking at the bigger picture, thinking strategically, and creating a vision. Leaders do the work of developing the company and helping individuals and teams reach their full potential by motivating, inspiring, and energizing them. Sometimes, that rocks the boat, especially when good staff move on to a different organization.

When we act only as either managers or leaders for too long, we create a void. Yes, we need to stabilize, but we also need to keep moving. Staying still too long makes us stagnant. On the other hand, always racing forward can lead to no foundation to build on. Focusing only on the future can create chaos, as we spin out of control.

Leaders must switch back and forth between manager and leader roles. Your strength may be seeing an employee's future potential, so you focus on that during their performance review. You talk to them about their goals and help them decide what training to take over the next year. You may also need to talk about them being late with paperwork; that conversation manages day-to-day challenges, which stabilizes their work and its effect on the rest of the team.

Many of us focus on getting the work right in front of us done first. It is the squeaky wheel demanding our attention, so, on the surface level, it appears to be what we are supposed to do. But if we only focus here, we miss a bigger picture that needs our attention.

When you set your sights farther down the road, you gain perspective. That big-picture view helps you realize that the urgent email isn't as urgent as it appears. It lets you see how completing a different task is more aligned with the program's overall growth.

If you've been avoiding making and communicating a hard decision, you may need to put your leadership hat on and think for a bit. Decisiveness, the ability to make a decision quickly and effectively, is a mental process, which means you, as the leader, need time to think through the decisions. The problem is that rather than being decisive, many leaders are wishy-washy, saying things such as

- "I need a couple more days to think about that."
- "I am just looking for a little bit more information."
- "What do you think?"

Do you hear it? That indecisiveness can leave your employees feeling unsafe, unstable, unclear, and directionless. They may feel as if no one is leading them.

Remember, a leader takes people in a direction. Management is holding the boat stable, ensuring the boat doesn't tip over with policies and procedures in place, paperwork done, *t*'s crossed, and *i*'s dotted. Managing absolutely must be done. People want to get paid. People want to know when their shift is scheduled. People want contracts signed. All of that is management. But they also need you to make decisions and communicate them.

A good way to decide whether you should lead or manage is to ask yourself, "Do I need to steady things, or do I need to rock the boat? Am I trying to stay where we are and create stability, or am I trying to take people someplace?" These questions help you to intentionally choose between your management and leadership hats.

Another important leadership lesson you may have missed is why engagement is critical to move your team toward a magnetic workplace. Let me give you the Coles Notes version.

Character Driven Leaders Create Engagement

When you lead with strong character, you create engagement with your people. And yes, you need an engaged team! Gallup defines engaged employees as those who are involved in, enthusiastic about, and committed to their work and workplace. They are engaged in their work, the people they work with, and the difference they are making.

Employee engagement reflects the involvement and enthusiasm of employees in their work and workplace. That engagement happens when you lead effectively and create loyal followers. Effective leaders

- have high levels of engagement with their team

- have the trust and respect of their team (which doesn't mean they always agree with them)

- bring purpose and meaning to the work the team is doing together

Remember earlier I said that Gallup's research has identified that managers account for at least 70 percent of the variance in employee engagement scores. That means if you have a group of unengaged employees, their low levels could rise if a new manager came in or if the current manager changed their style.

You might be wondering how to create an engaged team that trusts you while doing meaningful work together. To answer that, consider a leader you admire, believe in, and follow. What do you admire about them? My guess is that it isn't their title or accomplishments but the type of person they are. You might say they lead with integrity, have the courage to be honest, are decisive, or are good at motivating and inspiring the team. We admire and trust leaders with character.

Those words—"integrity," "courage," "honest," "decisive," "motivating," and "inspiring"—can describe character traits. They are ways leaders act, behave, and communicate that impact you. When they get it right, you trust them. When they don't, you might slander them on social media, gossip about them at the smokers' corner, or complain about them to your spouse or friends.

Leaders with strong character and engaged teams—teams that want to work together, do the work, and enjoy the work—have created a magnetic working environment.

I believe there are four fundamentals that help you be that type of leader. When you keep these in mind as you grow your character, you'll increase your team's engagement, moving it from toxic or tolerable to magnetic.

The Fundamentals of Leadership

It's possible you missed learning the fundamentals of leadership because you rose through the ranks quickly, had to step into management on the job, or your boss didn't know them either. Whatever the reason, to help you learn to do the work of leadership, here are my four fundamentals:

1   **Be yourself:** Lead your nonprofit with authenticity.
2   **Develop yourself:** Continuously grow yourself personally and professionally.
3   **Take care of yourself:** Be a balanced leader.
4   **Teach others to do the same:** Be a leader, teacher, mentor, and coach.

Later in the book, we'll cover strategies for implementing each of these fundamentals. But first, let's explore these concepts further so you can learn to master these fundamental nonprofit leadership strategies.

1. Be Yourself

Authentic leadership begins with embracing our unique selves. Too often, we feel pressured to conform to societal expectations or mimic the masculine leadership styles of our counterparts. As a result, we feel like we are armouring up, suiting up, or covering up our true selves. It's more than just the clothes we wear: it's the style, approach, and manner we bring to our leadership.

To be our best selves, we need to do the inner work of unmasking ourselves, shedding the armour, and embracing our genuine selves. That starts with identifying our values, beliefs, strengths, and quirks and learning to be comfortable with all of them.

When my client Sarah first came to me, she struggled with feelings of inadequacy and self-doubt. Having recently been promoted to a leadership position in her nonprofit organization, she felt pressure to project an image of confidence and authority. Yet, beneath the surface, she struggled with imposter syndrome, fearing she didn't have what it took to lead effectively. Through our coaching sessions and her self-reflective work, Sarah began to understand that her self-doubt was rooted in a lack of leadership training and a fear that her true personality wasn't the right fit for her position.

As we unpacked her strengths, gifts, and talents, she realized that who she was at her core was what would make her a strong leader. When she started to own her uniqueness, she embraced her authenticity and used it to lead with positive results.

Previously, Sarah had hesitated to express her emotions; however, she discovered that embracing vulnerability and empathy enhanced her leadership and resonated with her team. Sarah learned to leverage her emotions effectively, transforming her sensitivity from a perceived weakness into a strength.

By prioritizing self-reflective work, staying true to herself, and leading with integrity, Sarah gained the respect and trust of her colleagues, and she fostered a more collaborative and enjoyable work environment.

Being yourself is all about being you, through and through. It is about understanding your personality, getting acquainted with your strengths, and using them with intention. Being yourself also means learning to define your values, ethics, and morals and leading and living in alignment with them. Do the work to really get to know who you are so you can be yourself as you lead.

Later you'll learn about the strengths assessments I do with my students and clients and how you can do them too. I also ensure my clients dive deep into naming, defining, and learning to use their values. They often do this via a course called Values Verification, which is the first course I recommend to students who join as Training Library members. Inside the Training Library, women leaders have access to on-demand courses to help them lead with confidence, competence, composure, and with their integrity intact. You can find out more on my website kathyarcher.com/library.

In the Values Verification course, students narrow their values from a list of one hundred down to three. They often group word strings together into one defining value. They then define it and learn how to honour their values and align their decisions, priorities, and behaviours with what they value.

2. Develop Yourself

Continuous learning and growth are essential components of effective leadership. In the world of nonprofits, you spend most of your time learning the work, not the skills and inner growth necessary for impactful leadership. Strong and authentic leaders commit to ongoing personal and professional development. They have a growth mindset and a plan for developing themselves internally and tactically in their day-to-day work.

Another client of mine, Maria, was eager to prove herself and make an impact when she first stepped into her leadership role. However, she quickly realized that she lacked the necessary skills and knowledge to navigate the complexities of her new position.

I helped Maria develop her personal and professional development plan—her Character Development Plan—which focused on honing her leadership skills, developing emotional intelligence, and increasing her understanding of her strengths and talents. Maria grew into her leadership role through books, podcasts, and lessons in the Training Library. She embraced feedback as an opportunity for growth and sought mentors who could offer her guidance and support. As a result, she became more confident in her abilities and more effective in leading her team in the mission-driven work of their nonprofit organization.

Intentionally developing yourself is critical to becoming the leader you want to be. If you value your growth and development, you'll develop a plan for it. Ensure you make time every week for that personal and professional development work.

3. *Take Care of Yourself*

Leadership can be demanding, both mentally and physically. As leaders, we must prioritize our well-being to ensure we have the energy and resilience to tackle challenges head-on. Self-care isn't selfish; it's essential for sustaining our leadership effectiveness and preventing burnout. Self-care is critical in maintaining composure, focusing, and being decisive. After all, you can't pour from an empty cup. Strong leaders develop practical strategies for ensuring their minds and bodies are well equipped to handle the demands of leadership.

Juggling multiple responsibilities and deadlines, Lana had neglected her own needs in favour of serving others. She was a people pleaser and had trouble saying no. She was becoming exhausted and overwhelmed. As her energy levels waned and her stress levels soared, she realized she could not continue leading effectively without taking care of herself.

Together, we explored applying the Wellness AT Work course from the Training Library and developing basic self-care strategies. Lana knew she needed to practise setting boundaries and saying no more frequently so she had time to breathe between meetings, time to think, and time to take care of herself.

As Lana began prioritizing her well-being throughout her workday, she noticed a remarkable shift in her leadership style. She became more patient, compassionate, and resilient, inspiring her team to do the same. And she was so excited to have more energy left at the end of the day for the rest of her life.

I want to highlight the connection between your emotional stability and your physical well-being. Lisa Feldman Barrett uses the

Self-care is critical in maintaining composure, focusing, and being decisive. After all, you can't pour from an empty cup.

analogy of a budget to explain how our body's well-being connects to our emotions. She tells us, "Your brain's main job is to budget the internal resources of your body like water and salt and glucose and hormones and so on to keep you alive and well." As Barrett explains, emotions are predictions that our brains make based on our body budget status. When our brain predicts that energy needs will change, it prepares by adjusting our body budget, which can result in different emotional states. This is why when you are tired, hungry, or stressed, you may have less capacity to manage your emotions, because your brain is budgeting all its resources to keep your body physically stable.

When you are intentional about your wellness, it becomes more than self-care activities squeezed in. A mindset shift to wellness helps you see how your energy levels fuel you for leadership. You see how taking a few minutes to practise mindfulness before a tough meeting will help you feel composed. You'll realize that going for a run is what you need to clear your head so you can devise a strategy for the big problem you are facing.

4. Teach Others to Do the Same

True leaders empower those around them to embrace authenticity, continuous growth, and self-care. It starts with you though. You can only teach it effectively if you do it. When you help others unmask, develop, and care for themselves, it creates an engaged culture of loyal team members.

Inspiring leaders do more than manage their teams. Effective leaders learn to motivate, coach, and mentor their team members. True leadership is about empowering others to reach their full potential by supporting them, sharing knowledge, and helping them grow and thrive.

Sonya decided to embrace this principle wholeheartedly. Recognizing the importance of investing in her team's development, she implemented a system of supervision that focused not only on projects and clients but also on staff's personal and professional development. Sonya used a template from a course in the Training Library to ensure she followed up with one team member on her project of updating job descriptions, another on finishing up preparations for accreditation, and a third staff's in-progress certification. Sonya took an interest in how they were growing and demonstrated that interest by having regular conversations during their one-on-one supervisions.

By fostering a culture of growth and development, Sonya empowered her team members to excel in their roles. She cultivated a team who was excited to grow, be accountable, and learn to use their skills and talents to the fullest.

Sonya worked through the courses with me to help her embrace this fundamental. She learned how to give staff recognition that lands and how to have comfortable coaching conversations with her employees. She also began to have consistent one-on-one supervision that ensured their development; growth became an item on the agenda for their regular meetings.

When you work on those fundamentals—learning to be your authentic self, doing the personal development work, taking care of yourself and teaching others to do the same—you are doing the work of leading to develop engagement and the reputation you desire.

You might be saying, "Yes, that all sounds nice, but I'm busy, have a lot of work to do, and am always afraid of dropping the ball on something. I don't have time to do all of those things." I hear you loud and clear. But here's the thing: it is not just what you do but how you do it that grows your character. Effective leaders are good at tuning into their thoughts, recognizing which thoughts aren't helping them be their best, and then changing those thoughts. They set boundaries even when they initially feel uncomfortable. They take extra time to talk to their employees about their development, even if it means not attending a meeting others might deem important, because they have worked to align their priorities with their values, vision, and goals.

You are juggling a lot! The key is awareness of *what* you are juggling. When you develop your Character Development Plan, you'll still have to keep your eye on all the balls but in a more balanced way. There are three main balls I believe you should be juggling; here's what juggling them effectively means for a character driven leader.

Don't Juggle the Wrong Balls

The problem is you are juggling way too many balls, often the wrong ones, and you can't keep your eye on all of them. To lead effectively and with your integrity intact, you need to keep your focus on three main balls. This metaphor of juggling only three balls helps you decide how to prioritize tasks by aligning your actions with your desired identity.

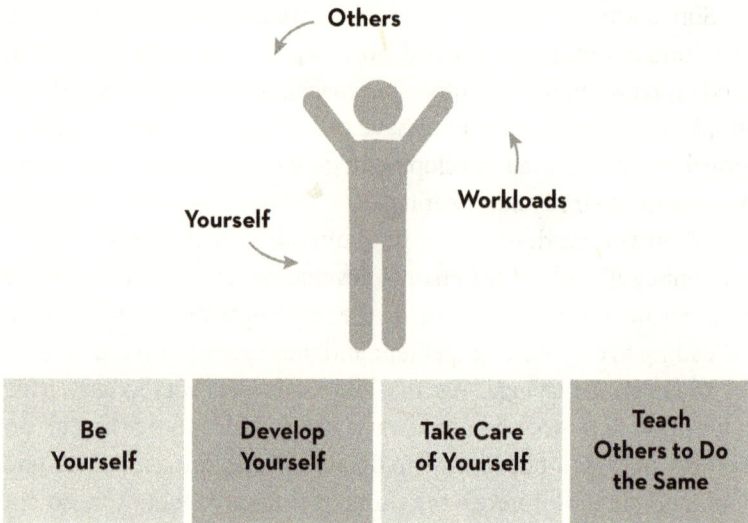

| Be Yourself | Develop Yourself | Take Care of Yourself | Teach Others to Do the Same |

Ball 1: Yourself

To effectively manage others, you must first learn to manage yourself. This aligns with the first three fundamentals of leadership: be yourself, develop yourself, and take care of yourself. To help you think about all you've got going on with the "me ball," concentrate on your essence, emotions, and energy.

What do I mean by "essence"? Your essence is the core of who you are as a leader. It encompasses your values, strengths, and character traits. It's your identity and how you define yourself. Understanding your essence is integral for aligning your actions with your principles and leading authentically.

Not embracing who I was often got me into trouble, and it's why I was not leading with integrity. I made this mistake because I thought what many leaders think: there's a right way to lead, and I thought I was doing it wrong.

Most of the role models for leadership in my life had been men. That's the way it is for the majority of us. Even if we are learning to lead from reading, most leadership books were written by men, many of them decades ago. The world has changed dramatically since many of these books were written. And while there's an incredible amount of wisdom and knowledge out there, as women, we're different and the world is different.

I believe we're just hardwired differently; that's the truth of the matter. And some of those things that we've tried to shut off, like our emotions, actually help us be more effective leaders. But of course, that concept is only making it into books now, and many of our leaders and mentors haven't learned it yet either.

When we try to emulate masculine role models, we learn about what to wear, how to act, what to say or not say, and how to *not* express emotions. Their style perhaps doesn't match who we are at our core.

I'm a friendly and chipper person, and I get along with people easily. When I tried to push that aspect of myself down, I felt that loss of integrity, and when I acted like an all-business kind of leader, it didn't feel right. And it didn't work out very well either. I had to bring empathetic relationship building into who I was as a leader because that gives me strength. That's what gives me the ability to lead well.

It was the same for Madeline, a client of mine who struggled with authenticity in her leadership role. Madeline believed she needed a more assertive and authoritative persona if she wanted to be taken seriously as a leader. However, through self-reflection and coaching, Madeline discovered her true strength lay in her empathy and compassion. By embracing her essence and leading from her authentic self, Madeline gained her team's respect and fostered a culture of trust and collaboration. Just like Madeline, you'll get a lot more comfortable embracing your essence as you do the work you set out to do in your Character Development Plan.

The other part of the "me ball" that you are juggling has to do with your own energy. Managing your energy is crucial to sustaining your leadership journey, as we talked about earlier in the fundamentals of leadership. As a nonprofit leader, you have a busy schedule, but you must balance your energy throughout the day by practising wellness, taking breaks, eating well, and shifting your focus to maintain your stamina. Managing your energy allows you to show up as the best version of yourself professionally and personally.

Leadership isn't a sprint; it is a marathon that never ends. Managing your energy is crucial for long-term success, so you can sustain your performance and avoid burnout. By prioritizing energy management, you'll maximize your productivity, creativity, and overall well-being, allowing you to lead with passion and purpose.

Ball 2: Others

I often discuss the balance between tasks and relationships, or projects and people, with my clients. Some tend to lean heavily on the do, do, do part: attending meetings and firing off emails. Those of us who do that too much miss the relationship component with our employees, which is critical for building engagement and trust.

Maybe you do what I used to do. I'd hop into a meeting and start talking about clients, reports, and projects without even checking in with the person in front of me. Remember when we talked about the differences between leaders and managers? I was missing the opportunity to be intentional about seeing my team members' potential and helping them get there.

To help you keep your eye on the "others ball," here are three essential focuses: care about them, give them direction, and help them get there.

Let's talk about *care*. We need to care about our people and let them know they matter to us and that we think they're an important part of our organization. One of the twelve statements that Gallup uses to measure team engagement is "My supervisor, or someone at work, seems to care about me as a person." That's what your employees want from you as a leader: they want to know you care about them. They don't want to feel like they're just a number, a warm body, or a person filling a seat.

For them to feel cared about, you must invest time, energy, and focus into making them feel like human beings, like they matter. This doesn't mean you only focus on them for an entire one-on-one conversation. It means that part of that conversation focuses on them. And when you're talking about other things, you bring that aspect of them into it.

Another way to make it about them is to *give them direction*. I know that they know what their job requires of them. But do they really? Sometimes, we need to be reminded. The number one question on Gallup's engagement survey is "Do I know what is expected of me at work?" Gallup suggests that kind of clarity is a basic fundamental need. In truth, sometimes our people don't know what is expected of them. Sometimes they have never been taught, or in the case of a group I met with the other day, expectations change every time a new leader comes in.

Nonprofits often bring people in quickly and complete new hire orientations as swiftly as possible. However, they are not as thorough as they need to be. Sometimes employees only get a couple of hours of on-the-job training or, if they are lucky, a full day. But two, three, or four weeks of shadowing, training, and mentoring? Not a chance.

Do we come back and check in? Do we review the orientation checklist again two, three, or four weeks after hiring a new employee? What about two or three months into it to see where they're at? Honestly, some people don't know what they're doing.

It's not only at orientation. Things change. Do we keep checking in to ensure we are providing enough direction and support? Sometimes, our employees need more direction than we've given them. And in the long run, it makes your juggling job easier if they have it.

Finally, *help them get there*. This component is about encouraging them. If you've taken the time to see them as people, you may know their strengths, their career direction, and what they want to learn. Your investment in them shows, and you need to also encourage and support them. Sometimes, you need to coach, train, and mentor them. You need to develop them, and that takes time and energy.

In nonprofits, we've sent team members to mandatory courses, like first aid, mental health first aid, and Indigenous cultural awareness. But I'm talking about training beyond that—training that they aspire to do. This isn't just about the organization and the position they're in today. I want you to see them as a person with a whole career ahead of them. Where are they going? They may not be with your organization forever. Some leaders try to hang on to their people when they've indicated they are ready to move on. Those people get bored or stuck in a position they've outgrown, soon becoming disgruntled employees.

Get curious about where they're going. Have that conversation. They don't need to tell you everything. But you need to see them as individuals and help them develop their career path, not just in their current position.

When you invest in them this way, they're going to think, "Hey, this leader cares about me. They care about my development. They care about my life. They care about my career journey. I feel like I matter." When that happens, that sense of trust is developed. That creates the engagement that I've been talking about. Do this and you will have an employee who's more loyal, effective, and engaged.

Ball 3: Workloads

The final ball you are juggling is the actual work you are all doing. You have three concerns here:

1   You need to manage the projects for which you and your team are responsible. Who does what?

2   You need to manage *your* priorities, and look beyond putting out fires and dealing with whatever crisis shows up, by being intentional and conscious about what's important but not yet urgent. What gets done first?

3   You need to manage the pace of the work. How fast do I need it done?

A leader's reputation can be significantly impacted if they struggle to manage tasks, workloads, and priorities effectively. You've seen such leaders! They are perceived as disorganized, indecisive, or lacking in direction, which leads to their team members losing trust in and respect for them.

An inability to prioritize tasks and allocate resources efficiently can result in missed deadlines and decreased productivity, and if this is you, your staff will be annoyed, frustrated, and stressed, which leads to a toxic team. When our program grew so fast, I struggled to juggle both my and my team's workloads. My reputation as a capable leader became tarnished, and that affected the morale within my team. They were tired of being pushed, pulled, and dragged to get more done than they reasonably could and criticized when they didn't.

My inability to handle tasks, workloads, and priorities eroded my credibility and hindered my ability to both keep the boat stable and move it forward. I got mired in the muck and got stuck. If only I'd had my own curriculum and the Infinite Leadership Loop then!

To maintain a strong reputation and lead with your strength of character, it's essential to balance driving projects forward, supporting staff members in their roles, and caring for your own well-being. How do you do that? By setting clear expectations and delegating tasks effectively, we can prevent burnout and ensure everyone's contributions align with organizational goals. But it's easier said than done.

When we aren't managing workloads intentionally, we are whacking moles! In the fast-paced world of nonprofit leadership, it's easy to fall into a cycle of reacting, constantly putting out fires without pausing to prioritize effectively. The key to breaking free from this cycle is to shift from a mindset of constant reaction to recognition that you choose what to tackle next and you can be intentional in decision-making. To avoid constantly whacking moles, you must pause and consciously choose where to invest your time, energy, and focus.

You now know the differences between management and leadership and why you must balance those aspects of your role. You better understand the fundamentals of leadership and the three balls you are juggling. This knowledge may already make you feel a bit more equipped to lead with your strength of character. But knowing and doing are two different things.

With your better understanding of character, emotions, and leadership, it's time to look at how to lead with authenticity and integrity while finding balance so you have energy left for the rest of your life. Because let's be honest, that's probably what's been neglected most. We'll start with five steps to strengthen your character.

PART TWO

HOW TO STRENGTHEN YOUR CHARACTER

5

Developing Character Awareness and Essential Leadership Traits

ERHAPS, LIKE I WAS, you aren't happy with what you see in the mirror today. The second time I hit a big leadership low, I was very aware that I didn't like where I was, the person I'd become, or the lack of impact I was having. And I certainly didn't like going to work every day. I felt stuck and didn't know how to change it.

With the help of my coach, I learned that our personality and, yes, our character, are not static—at least, they don't have to be. You can change and shape the person you are. Shaping your identity happens when you develop a new vision of your future self. When I learned that, I saw how I could shape my character and my life in a more aligned way. I began to ask myself questions like the following:

- How do I lead with integrity?
- How do I become a respected leader?
- How do I inspire my team?

- How do I feel good about myself and the work I do?
- How do I balance work with my whole life?

Regularly contemplating these questions began to shape the leader I wanted to be. This self-reflective work was crucial to my character development. Character development is the personal and professional development work of leadership. Inner work is required to grow yourself. You cannot intentionally choose what's best for you and be that person until you stop and look at who you want to be.

You may think you don't have time or space for it. I used to think I would have to go away to a meditation retreat, sit alone on some hill, or become deeply spiritual to do that. All of that may help. However, day-to-day self-reflection makes the most significant shifts, albeit in small daily increments. Let's get started. It's your turn to do the self-reflective work of developing your character.

The Steps for Developing Your Character

Here are the steps for developing your character:

1 Increase your awareness of how your character develops.

2 Get to know your character strengths and your values, ethics, and morals.

3 Create a vision of your aspirational identity.

4 Create your plan for getting there with a Character Development Plan.

5 Build a system of ongoing self-reflection, feedback, practice, and then more reflection, feedback, and practice with the Infinite Leadership Loop.

In this chapter, we will look at steps 1 and 2. In the next chapter, we will get to step 3 and build your aspirational identity. Following that, you'll learn how to create your Character Development Plan.

In part three, you'll dive deeper into learning how to use the Infinite Leadership Loop. Finally in the last section, you will learn six practices to help make it stick.

Increase Your Awareness of How Your Character Develops

As with any change, awareness is always the first step.

Character development has its own language, as we explored earlier in the book. You first need to familiarize yourself with the language of character and how the words "values," "virtues," "character traits," and "character strengths" all fit together and apply to your life.

We often use the word "values" when we mean "virtues." Values are your goals or the way you aspire to live. We may value our family, but that doesn't mean we spend as much time with them or treat them as we aspire to. We may value our health but still eat donuts and chocolate bars and drink too many lattes. We interchange words that have multiple meanings: valuing honesty, being honest once, and being an honest person are all different things.

Identifying your values is the first step, but it doesn't end there. You must then learn how to bring that value to life and operationalize it. When you honour your values with your daily actions, you live virtuously or with virtue.

So, where does character fit in? It's kind of in the middle. To become a person who lives with virtue and honours their values, you need tools or pathways. Your character traits are your pathways. In fact, you may use many character traits to achieve a certain virtue. Character traits are methods for practising your values, and building your character is the path to virtuous living. Think of a virtue as your habitual way of responding and behaving. We all encounter the same situations, and how we habitually react to those situations defines who we are.

"Character" is not often discussed in leadership training, nor are "virtues." But character and virtues go hand in hand. Virtuous living and leading are the outcomes of consistently practising your character traits. Virtuous action includes your intentional habits, ways of being, and behavioural patterns.

We move from valuing something to acting on that value. To act on it, we must use certain traits, such as curiosity, courage, or compassion. The more consistently we use those traits, the more they define our character. If I am curious only occasionally, I would not be considered a curious person. But if I am frequently curious, people would expect it from me and call me curious. The key is consistency.

Think about character and virtue in the context of leadership. Honesty is a trait. We want our leaders to be honest instead of hiding things, sharing partial truths, or being downright deceptive. Honesty creates trust. But what if you are honest only sometimes? Does that make you an honest leader? Would people describe you as being honest? Would they say they could trust you to be honest? Or might they say that you choose to be honest when it suits you, which makes you untrustworthy, sneaky, or even weak?

However, if you consistently practised being honest, not cruel and hurtful, but authentic, genuine, forthright, and sincere, might others describe you as honest? Would they say that while your answer isn't always the one they want to hear, they can trust you to be accurate, truthful, and straight up?

A consistent habit of practising honesty influences others to see you as living with the virtue of courage. You have the courage to share hard but truthful messages. You are brave when giving genuine feedback.

The opposite of a virtue is a vice, which arises when we overuse or underuse a virtue. Let's take the trait of honesty again. Overusing honesty could mean sharing blunt and hurtful but still accurate observations; underusing honesty would mean being inauthentic or phony.

When you give feedback to your employees about their interactions with a client, you may temper your comments to get your point across and not put them on the defensive. Instead of saying, "You need to stop towering over clients when you talk to them. It's no wonder they don't want to cooperate with you," you dial in your honesty by saying, "I noticed you were trying hard to get your client to understand your point. Perhaps sitting beside them as you communicated would have helped you create a feeling of cooperation."

Aristotle says virtue is a disposition or a tendency, not a faculty or power of the mind, like memory, reason, or speech. I may feel angry, loving, or generous. I then have the capacity to express that feeling in a variety of ways. That capacity is my faculty. The question is, Do you use it? I have the power or capacity to withhold my anger, but will I?

- Am I a loose cannon when I get angry, or am I inclined to express anger effectively?

- What is my habit of responding in moments that feed my anger?

- What can typically be expected from me when I experience anger?

I have the power to offer to help someone. I have that capacity. But what is my disposition or propensity? Or, to put it another way, how do I typically behave when given the opportunity to offer help to someone?

- Do I have a habit of holding the door for others?

- Am I inclined to offer to help my co-workers when it's clear they are overwhelmed?

- What can typically be expected from me when I am around people who could use a helping hand?

By choosing to use my faculties, or my mind, to act in ways that allow me to live and lead with virtue, I build my character. As I've said, character is developed over time. We chisel it out of ourselves. Character is developed through a series of actions that, when we are consistent, allow us to become a person living with a certain virtue.

Let's walk through some examples of virtuous behaviour, first going a bit deeper into honesty.

When people hear what their leader says they value and then see their leader's actions match their words, **they believe in their leader's strong integrity.**

Honesty as a Value: I Think Honesty Is Important

Just because I think honesty is important, I may not necessarily practise honesty or be seen as an honest person. This is an important distinction. The disconnect between our values and behaviours causes us to experience frustration, find ourselves out of balance, and feel conflicted. We often know something is important to us but don't act on it.

For example, you may believe that it is important to do quality work. Yet due to your overwhelming workload, you tend to rush things and feel you are not doing your best. Valuing quality work does not mean your actions are aligned with that value.

Honesty as a Character Trait: I Practise Honesty

I work to tell the truth when I can. We can be honest in some but not all contexts. I may be honest at home or when working with a particular group or person. However, in other teams or in some relationships, I may tend to fudge the truth, hold back information, or mislead.

Perhaps you are honest about what is happening in your organization. You are transparent about upcoming changes and budgets. You authentically share your concerns about how something will impact the team. However, you may not be so honest about the brownie you snuck at lunch, how tired you really are, or who you are planning to let go.

To practise honesty, you may rely on many other traits, such as courage, compassion, and spirituality. You may want to be honest with someone but know it will be a tough conversation. To engage in that dialogue, you must use courage to step forward. As you share that tough message, you may also express compassion when the person on the receiving end reacts. Before engaging in the conversation, you may say a prayer asking for strength, guidance, and the ability to stay composed. These are all tools to assist you in acting on your value of honesty.

Honesty as a Virtue: I Am Honest

People know I am an honest person. Regardless of the situation, I can be counted on to be honest. That doesn't mean I am rude, hurtful, or insensitive. I may choose when to share honest messages or find ways to share truths with those who need to hear them, but I am honest.

Here's an example. If you are experiencing cutbacks, you will share that information with the team as soon as it is confirmed. Before that, you may have shared the rumour with the leadership team. You weren't "completely transparent," knowing part of your job is about maintaining team morale and planning strategically.

When you tell the team, you are upfront about the details you have and sincere about what you still have yet to confirm. Your straightforwardness leaves your team feeling "in the know" and taken care of. It may be clear that there will be layoffs, but people don't get the sense you are hiding anything. You, too, feel that you have been genuine and on the up and up with your team. It won't make the final cuts any easier. You probably care deeply about these people. However, you won't feel pulled out of alignment with your value of honesty.

Here are some more examples to help you understand why consistency is an important part of character building.

Integrity as a Value	I Think Integrity Is Important
	I notice and often judge others as not being in integrity.
	I feel out of alignment when I don't act with integrity
Integrity as a Character Trait	I Practise Being in Integrity
	I try to align my values with my actions.
	I try to do what I say I will do.

Integrity as a Virtue	**I Am a Person of Integrity**
	My words and actions match.
	I follow through on what I say I will do.

Respect as a Value	**I Think Respect Is Important**
	I think we should treat women and men equally in leadership.
Respect as a Character Trait	**I Practise Respecting Others**
	I practise being respectful of genders when I hire.
Respect as a Virtue	**I Am a Respectful Person**
	I am known as being a leader who is inclusive of gender and culture.

Knowledge and Learning as a Value	**I Think Knowledge and Learning Are Important**
	I think everyone should have the right to further their education.
Knowledge and Learning as Character Traits	**I Practise Increasing My Knowledge**
	I regularly take online courses and training seminars.
Knowledge and Learning as a Virtue	**I Am a Wise, Knowledgeable, and Intellectual Person**
	I am known to be a lifelong learner.

By understanding the nuances of character building, you'll be better able to cultivate your own character with intention. More than creating a list of words you wish to emulate, you'll understand how to live that list.

Key Character Traits for Effective Leadership

As you create your aspirational identity in step 3, there are many traits you may want to develop in yourself, but you may also wonder which are most important for leaders. The answer is that whatever traits are the most *you* are the most important. Be sure to place these at the top of your Character Development Plan. Both Clifton-Strengths and VIA Character Strengths (which you'll learn more about in part 3) have discovered that when you use your top traits, you are more likely to be engaged, contribute meaningfully, experience a greater sense of well-being and happiness, and succeed in various aspects of your life. The bottom line is that being you is best.

In addition to the traits that make you feel most authentic, there are some traits you may want to cultivate to be more successful in leadership, even if they are not your top traits. Here are three that I believe are essential to effective leadership.

1. Integrity

Integrity is the sense you can be trusted, and it's the number one trait people want in their leaders. And as Neale Donald Walsch says, "[Highly evolved beings] do not tell the truth. [Highly evolved beings] are the truth." It's not just our words: it's our actions and whether they align with what we say. We want our leaders to do what they say they will do, walk their talk, and be true to their word.

When you are in integrity, you act according to your beliefs and adhere to moral and ethical standards. When you lack integrity, things are incongruent. What you say and what you do don't match.

The word "integrity" comes from the same root as "integer," a whole number. We lead with integrity when we are whole, aligned, and congruent. We need to align our ethics and morals with our behaviours. Your ethics are what is important to you. They are what you stand for, what you believe in, your principles, and your values. Your morality is conforming to those principles. It is what you do, and it's how you act. It is your behaviours and attitudes.

- You believe in honesty, but are you always honest?

- You value accuracy, but do you ensure accuracy in your own work and your team's?

- You say your clients come first, but do they really?

When your professed values are misaligned with your actual conduct, not only does a sense of inner conflict arises, but the people around you feel it. This erodes your integrity. When you fall out of integrity, you might have a pattern of excuses and be inconsistent. For example, you might be on time for some meetings, but a pattern emerges of being late when things get busy.

Your inconsistencies might show up in how you do things depending on who is around or who is watching. For example, you may come to meetings on time when the big boss is there but are regularly late at other times. Or you watch your words closely when certain people are around but lose your cool when they are not.

When people hear what their leader says they value and then see their leader's actions match their words, they believe in their leader's strong integrity. They know they can lean on their leader, count on them, and trust them. Therefore, our goal as leaders is to gain the trust of our team by working toward integrating what we believe and what we do.

Integrity is about patterns and habits. When you are in integrity, you have unchanging standards. People trust you to do what you say you will do, even in tough times. The first step to leading with integrity is clearly understanding your beliefs, principles, values, ethics, and standards. You need to know:

- Where is the line?
- What hill will you die on?
- What won't you ever waiver on?
- What's not worth fighting about?

If you don't know what's important to you and why it's important, it's hard to live in alignment. Identifying what matters most to you—your values, ethics, and morals—is a fundamental step for character development.

2. Moral Courage

To lead as a character driven leader, your courage will come into play daily as you

- lead team meetings
- apply for grants or ask for funding
- take on a new program
- engage in a difficult conversation
- ask for a wage increase, apply for a new position, or tell your boss what you need

All of those actions demonstrate courage, but unlike the courage required to bungee jump or walk on the glass floor of the Grand Canyon observation deck, courage in leadership is less about daring acts. It's about the day-to-day decisions you make.

There are two types of courage: physical and moral. Physical courage as defined by Olivier Serrat is "fortitude in the face of death (and its threat), hardship, or physical pain." I took adult swimming lessons, and I remember standing on the edge of the pool and jumping into the deep end. That required physical courage. Let me tell you, it did not compare to the courage I needed when I had to let an employee go. That required moral courage.

Serrat defines moral courage as "the strength to use ethical principles to do what one believes is right even though the result may not be to everyone's liking or could occasion personal loss." Moral courage is what we need when, a month before Christmas, we know we have to cut a program but feel deep compassion for the program's employees. When our values, beliefs, and ethics are put to the test, often colliding with one another, we must summon courage to take action. Moral courage is doing the right thing in the face of doubt, fear, or backlash.

A woman with moral courage is seen as a leader with integrity. That is because her actions align with what she says she believes in, what she communicates is important to the team, and what she holds onto firmly even when it's hard. That's the courage part. Integrity requires you to make tough decisions and tackle difficult tasks. It boils down to being aware of what is happening inside you and then managing it with your thoughts, feelings, and actions. It is acting with courage.

The opposite of moral courage, moral muteness, is allowing wrongdoings to go unchallenged or unreported. Being morally mute happens far more often than we think because we lack the courage to stand up. Ask yourself if you have the courage to take hard stands, make difficult decisions, and say what needs to be said when

- you might be ridiculed for your decision
- your reputation might be at risk
- you might lose your job

Rather than following the pack, doing it the way it's always been done, or taking the easy route, moral courage requires not only asking yourself what is important and right but also staying with that decision, even when it's very hard and there are risks associated with it.

Moral courage is knowing what is ethical and then acting on that awareness. To make moral decisions, you need to know your morals. To have moral courage, you must stand behind those moral decisions. It is the action part that requires courage.

Michael Josephson, who founded the Josephson Institute of Ethics, sums it up nicely: "Moral courage is the engine of integrity. It is our inner voice that coaxes, prods, and inspires us to meet our responsibilities and live up to our principles when doing so may cost us dearly." It's the inner voice that you must tune into via self-reflection to be the authentic leader you desire to be.

3. Hope

The absence of hope is hopelessness. When you have no positive expectations or optimism for the future, you may lead with cynicism, pessimism, and a tone of resignation. "Why bother? What's the point? This is just the way it is." It's a fast track to survival mode and a toxic workplace.

However, when faced with challenges in our nonprofits, we need a leader who sees a way through potential problems and obstacles. Your people need you to inspire a sense of hope through the work you do and the vision you have.

Where leaders sometimes go wrong is when they act like a relentlessly positive cheerleader, which comes across as inauthentic, disingenuous, or unbelievable. Your team needs genuine hope, which is made up of three components according to the hope theory developed by Charles R. Snyder.

First, hope is the belief that tomorrow will be better than today. Can you envision a better tomorrow? That's your goal or target, and you need to communicate this. Sometimes, we forget to share our vision for the future: the direction we are going in and the outcome we hope to achieve. We may have shared it once, but we must do it repeatedly.

Second, hope is an expectation that you can reach that goal. You need to have the confidence and agency to get there. Confidence starts with competence, so you need to communicate to your team why you are confident you can get there. Why do you believe it's possible? Again, leaders sometimes forget to share their thoughts on this. While leaders believe it, others haven't heard why they believe it.

Third, to be truly hopeful, you need to have a plan that includes multiple pathways. "If plan A doesn't work, we will try plan B. If plan B falls through ..." and so on. This is called pathways thinking.

To evaluate how hopeful you are about a particular change, ask yourself these questions that address the three parts of hope theory:

1 **Belief:** Do you believe that it's possible?

2 **Confidence:** Do you think you have the capacity to get there?

3 **Pathways Thinking:** Do you have a plan (and a backup plan) for how you will get there?

You need to communicate all three components to your team.

Think back to March 2020. As the pandemic began to grind things to a halt, so did the systems, policies, and practices of your organization. The way you had been doing things wasn't going to work anymore. Sending people home to work left them without the tools to perform their jobs. The expectations for masking were often unrealistic. The staffing shortage became dire as people got sick and needed to isolate. Quickly, a sense of hopelessness emerged.

Leaders who effectively navigated the pandemic, both non-profit and global leaders, demonstrated and communicated hope. Many of these successful leaders were women. They communicated that tomorrow would be better than today and explained why they thought that was possible, outlining what tools, resources, and pathways they would take to get there.

> "I know that working on your laptop eight hours a day is not good for your eyes and back. I'm hopeful we can get proper computer equipment for everyone working from home. I've got our IT person pricing it out and a call to the funder to address the need for emergency funding."

> "I get it. We are all running out of staff to fill shifts. At the inter-agency meeting, we talked about how we can staff our group homes in a way that meets client needs but also considers employees' needs, health, and families. We are looking at ways of moving clients around and sharing relief staff, and I'm hopeful we will have a plan by tomorrow afternoon."

Communicating all three aspects of hope is vital for your staff to trust you, believe you, and be inspired by your sense of hope. Ensure you don't stop at a vision of a more hopeful tomorrow. Your team needs you to tell them why you believe that is possible and how you'll make it so.

Integrity, moral courage, and hope are all character traits you need to build, but those three traits do not comprise an exhaustive list for leading with strength of character. You must look at who you are and who you are becoming. Let's move to that conversation.

6

Who Are You, and Who Are You Becoming?

EMEMBER OUR three character building questions? Steps two and three in character development are about getting to know yourself: embrace your essence and then ponder your potential.

Embrace Your Essence: Who Am I?

No journey can begin without a starting point. Rather than asking "Where am I now?" ask yourself, "Who am I now?"

As we entered adulthood, many of us shifted from trying to stand out as teens to accommodating what we thought was needed by the world around us. This unconscious socialization happens because we believe we must behave in a certain way to be accepted in a particular group. We know what is morally right and what is not and the rules we must follow to succeed. We have spent much of our lives trying to meet someone else's expectations of us. It's how we have survived, fit in, and gotten ahead. And that's okay. That's what got us here. But, to paraphrase Marshall Goldsmith, what got us here won't get us where we want to go.

Many of us have no idea who we are. We haven't slowed down enough to examine the person we are today and then decide which parts to keep and which need an upgrade. We avoid looking in the mirror except to critically judge our physical faults, missteps, and mistakes. Because we rarely take the opportunity to gaze into our own eyes and see the soul within, we've lost contact with who we are at our core. The real us is underneath the makeup, clothes, and psychological armour we wear daily. It's time to clean house and examine what's underneath all the layers we've amassed over the years.

Embracing your essence starts with looking at what shapes your current identity. Ask yourself:

- Who am I?
- What do I value?
- What are my beliefs?
- What are my strengths?
- What hills am I willing to die on?

These are the foundations for your current identity and the things you can change as you shape your future identity. To embrace your essence, you'll look at what's shaped you in your life and clarify your talent and character strengths, values, ethics, and morals, as well as your personality traits. More on that in a minute.

You'll also look and listen for feedback. You can specifically ask others, and you can look at what others have said about you in reviews and performance appraisals. Look at what people say about you in emails, cards, and notes. You might talk to people you trust and ask about your impact. Tune in to what others say. For example, people have always told me that my smile was a key feature. That lets me know it helps me connect. You are looking for themes in what people say about you.

Most importantly, you'll practise awareness through journaling and self-reflection. Though we will explore this further in part 4, throughout the book are many ideas for self-reflective exercises.

Take a Moment to Look at What Shaped You

What you've experienced in life unconsciously shapes who you are today. It may have shaped you in a way that is not helping you be your best today. It's important to look back at the things that have happened in our lives and the meaning we have attached to them. Take some time to review:

- Milestones

- Peak experiences

- Defining moments

- Childhood and adulthood experiences that stand out

- Genetic makeup including physical traits, characteristics, or disabilities

For example, when I look back at what has shaped me, I consider the following:

- I was raised on a farm.

- I was involved in Sunday school, Girl Guides, and 4-H.

- My mom worked at my school as an aide. She had close relationships with the teachers, one of whom was very tech savvy. I believe this shaped my mom's determination for my family to be among the first to get a Commodore 64 computer.

- I developed my work ethic by imitating my parents from a young age—babysitting, mowing lawns, cleaning for people, and doing janitorial work.

- My dad chose to courageously move away from his childhood home in Nova Scotia to Alberta and then brought my mom and my older sister out there. This was basically unheard of in my extended family, which meant I had very little contact with them growing up.

- My sister died when I was fourteen, and this hit our family hard. It was my first introduction to grief and loss.

- I ran away from home when I was seventeen, moved in with my boyfriend, and married him a year later. We are still married today, which is not the case for most seventeen-year-olds who move in with their boyfriends. Moreover, through that experience, I maintained a standard of excellence in school, attaining honour roll status, receiving achievement awards, and graduating college with distinction.

Each of these things, and many more, shaped who I am today. And what happened to you has shaped you. Author and commentator David Brooks says, "People don't see the world through their eyes, they see it with their entire life." Take time to look back at your entire life and consider how it created the view that you now look through.

You may want to create a timeline of your life. Visually mapping out your life allows you to gain a profound perspective on how you've come to be who you are today. I have the milestones of my life mapped out on flipchart paper. It's so informative. You are looking for themes and patterns. I can see my life has always had a different flow to it when I've been immersed in learning. Each time I take a big step in developing myself, I feel a shift in my identity.

Identify Your Strengths

Next, identify your strengths using various assessments. I encourage all of my students to complete the VIA Character Strengths profile. It helps you understand your character strengths. Many of my students also do the CliftonStrengths assessment, which helps you identify your talent strengths. The two assessments are different, but you'll often see overlapping themes. For example, love of learning is one of my top character traits on my VIA Character Strengths profile, and learner is my top talent on my CliftonStrengths assessment. This means learning comes naturally to me (essential, effortless, and energizing), and it's what I do best. There is a fee for the Clifton-Strengths assessment, but if you buy one of their books, some of which I recommend, you'll get a code to complete your top five for free. I am a certified CliftonStrengths coach, so if you want help with understanding your strengths, reach out to me.

Beyond the formal assessments, note what you already know you are good at, enjoy, or excel in. Add to that things you hear others say about you. Another way to identify core strengths is to look back to your youth. What were you doing then? What activities were you involved in, good at, or enjoyed? Here's an example from my own list.

- I was a reader from as early as I can remember (learner).

- I used to walk to the end of our lane and birdwatch at the lake (appreciation of beauty and excellence).

- I was involved in 4-H and received public speaking awards (public speaking).

- I was the president of my 4-H club and involved in the student council (leadership).

List Your Values, Morals, and Ethics

To identify your values, look at a big list of values. (You can find one at kathyarcher.com/cdlextras.html.) Narrow that list to ten words or groups of words that match your values. Take those ten and then narrow them down to three. Finally, take those three values and define them. What do they actually mean to you? In the Training Library, my students work through several self-reflective exercises to name, define, and operationalize their values and learn to use them to make value-based decisions. I also encourage them to come back at least annually and review. Values change, especially how we define them. For many, the importance of family and its definition will change from your twenties to your sixties.

Get clear on your morals, ethics, and beliefs. Take time to write down things you strongly believe in, things you are not willing to waver on, and the hills you will die on. You'll add to this list, building on it as you go. Combined with your values, this list will serve as your moral compass.

Embracing your essence is not done by completing an exercise or two. It is done by assessing, asking, and constantly going deeper through self-awareness. Hearing others tell me I'm always learning and seeing it appear on assessments as a strength doesn't mean I embrace it. Loving the parts of who we are that we've pushed down takes time.

As you take stock of your essence, you'll want to decide which parts of you you'd like to hold onto, which parts need to grow or mature, and what you'll need to add to become the person you want to be. In essence, you'll consider what's staying, what's going, and what are you growing in yourself. That takes us to pondering your potential and developing your aspirational identity. Too often, we've wondered, "How can I lead like others?" Now it's time to ask, "How can I lead more like myself?"

Ponder Your Potential: Who Am I Becoming?

When we examine who we are becoming, we aren't looking to find ourselves; we are creating ourselves. Instead of conforming and reacting to the world around us, we begin by making conscious choices to manage our lives, choose our character, and create our impact. The term for this is self-determining, or self-authoring. You are writing the next chapter of your life.

Having control over your own life and circumstances (to the extent that is possible) takes you out of survival mode and develops the character you desire. Pondering your potential allows you to do just that by looking deeply at yourself, seeing the person you want to become, and then creating that version of yourself. We start with what you discovered when you embraced your essence.

- You may have realized you are a caring and compassionate person in some areas of your life, but you seem to forget those traits at work most days.

- You've always said integrity and honesty are incredibly important to you, yet as you examined your current behaviour, you saw areas where your actions aren't matching your words.

- You may have observed how much more frequently you lose control of your emotions, snap, and speak in ways that are a bit too sharp, harsh, or biting.

In working with my coach, I realized I lacked integrity, not just because people said I did but because, through careful self-reflection, I saw it with my own heart.

- I said family was my most important value, but the hours I was putting into work and the state of my relationship with my family said otherwise.

- I told my staff I was there for them when they needed me, but my time away from the office, meeting schedule, and unresponsiveness conveyed a different message.

I wasn't walking my talk. I wasn't leading with integrity, and I decided it was time to change that. You may come to similar conclusions. That's when we start to look at our potential, our best selves, a new version of who we are, and we see what we need to do to get there. By pondering our potential, we set new intentions for who we are becoming. For example:

- I will be a caring leader with compassion for what my team is dealing with.

- I will be composed as I navigate the daily challenges of leadership.

- I will lead with integrity and honesty, building trusting relationships and walking my talk.

As we look to our future selves, we often worry that certain parts of us are forever etched into who we are. But there is an even larger portion of you that you can define, mould, and develop. Consider:

- Once a pessimist does not always make you a pessimist.

- If you've never been good at public speaking, you can learn to become an influential speaker.

- Just because you've always been a taskmaster, there's still potential to develop more balance between relationships and tasks.

- Even though your family is known for being hotheads, you can practise managing your anger and responses.

The nature versus nurture discussion reminds us that some of who we are results from our genes. Other parts of our personality and character have developed in response to our upbringing. However, a third component is often overlooked: choice. You get to choose who you want to be.

The challenge is that rather than choosing who to become, we often leave it up to chance. We allow life to weather us, scar us, and impact how others see our character. We act as if we don't have a choice. We've come to believe that life is hard and this is what happens as a result, that it's just the way it is. When we live with this fixed mindset, others begin to see us as a product of our pain and suffering. You've probably heard a woman described as a "bitter old lady." Is that where your current path is leading you? Will you choose a different path?

If you do not intentionally focus on who you are becoming, you become a product of your environment:

- If everyone around you is lazy on Fridays, you'll lose the work ethic your parents taught you so long ago—unless you intentionally hold tight to it.

- If you are not careful, you will become judgmental, always questioning, evaluating, and eyeing people up, just as your boss

You need an aspirational identity, a target or goal that helps you shape today's behaviour.

does. You will learn by osmosis—unless you deliberately choose another way.

- If you work in a toxic environment, you'll unconsciously learn the value of gossip with your ears perking up when you hear useful tidbits—unless you consciously choose a different path.

As you look back, you may wonder how things could have been any different based on what you've been through. For many of us, we've experienced traumatic events that have shaped our lives. But what if we see those through a different lens?

Post-Traumatic Growth

As you develop your Character Development Plan, you may want to examine how you will heal from trauma you've experienced in life and leadership. Some of you may want to skip over this section if you feel as though you haven't experienced trauma. I wonder, perhaps, if you have a perspective on trauma and about how bad it needs to be to be called "trauma." An event doesn't have to meet a certain threshold to count as trauma.

You can find assessments online in which you rate the number of stressful or traumatic events you've been through in the last few years. These ask you to indicate if you have experienced or witnessed things like life threats, sexual assault, or severe injuries. These are helpful gauges but rarely are they all encompassing, so they minimize the traumatic events we go through that may not be included.

For instance, I've never seen "being on a walk with your dog and having three dogs attack your dog" listed on any assessment. But that traumatic incident happened to me over ten years ago and still has profound effects on me when I'm walking, and any dog comes near me. Nor on those lists are having a grievance filed against you by your employees, which I know from personal experience can create extreme trauma. My client received a message about her that was not intended for her eyes. The comment was hurtful and mocked her lack of confidence; it still creates a wash of shame in her when she thinks about it. I could give you countless other examples of things that could be trauma-inducing, but I'm sure you have your own list.

Trauma happens when we experience an overwhelming amount of stress that exceeds our ability to handle it and the emotions that come with it. Dr. Benjamin Hardy reminds us that trauma isn't just the extreme manifestations we imagine, but "it includes any negative experience or incident that shapes who you are and how you operate in the world. We have all experienced and have been or are, impacted by trauma." I don't have to tell you that happens a lot in leadership.

Trauma makes you confused and insecure. We may feel angry, guilty, or full of shame. And if we don't deal with it, it lingers, sometimes for our entire lives, triggering us out of the blue and sending us spiralling again. As Dr. Benjamin Hardy says, "Trauma either traps you in the past or propels extreme transformation and growth." When we use trauma to grow, it is known as post-traumatic growth.

I had to take that experience of intense overwhelm, stress, shame, and anger when I lost the respect of my team and turn it around. I had to grow from it to move beyond the trauma. You see that in my work today and in this book. And I have seen clients move beyond trauma too.

One important way to move through trauma is to share your story. Gabor Maté, known for his groundbreaking work in the field of trauma healing, writes, "Trauma is not what happens to us. But what we hold inside in the absence of an empathetic witness." This is partly why support groups such as Alcoholics Anonymous work so well: they provide a space to share pain, shame, and trauma. Someone else witnesses it. It's not something you hide anymore. In fact, a common saying within the AA community is "You are only as sick as your secrets."

Over the years, many of my coaches, counsellors, and trusted friends have provided vital witnessing for me. Healing comes when you share your story and allow it to change. As part of a membership to the Training Library, my students can join me for a monthly call.

On many of those calls, we are witnessing each other's trauma which makes it easier to bear.

Changing your view of your past trauma allows you to change your view of your future self, creating a new you and a new identity.

Your Aspirational Identity

Your identity is how you define yourself. It is the narrative you have of yourself—not just who you are today but also how you see the way you were in the past and who you will be in the future. But we can change those identities: our past, present, and future selves.

Are you changing your personality? Yes, in fact, you are. Even though we long thought our personalities were static, research has revealed that they are malleable. Part of cultivating the character we desire is developing and maturing existing traits, as well as adopting personality traits we've never exhibited.

In *Personality Isn't Permanent*, a book I highly recommend you read, Dr. Benjamin Hardy argues that personality "can, should, and does change." He writes, "Your goals shape your identity, and your identity shapes your actions. And your actions shape who you are and who you are becoming. This is how personality is developed."

As you learn to develop your character, you'll continue to refine your narrative of yourself through self-reflective exercises. You'll change the lens on how you see your past, current, and future selves. We will talk about past traumatic experiences you've faced in leadership and change the way you view those stories through the lens of post-traumatic growth. You'll learn to use curiosity to mould those patterns of subconscious thoughts to move from surviving to thriving. That will in turn influence your workplace culture, shifting it away from toxic toward magnetic.

We are teleological beings. We function best with goals, deadlines, objectives, projects, ambitions, and aspirations. Therefore, we need a target for you to aspire to: the aspirational self you need to create. Your aspirational self is your image of yourself when you are at your best. The person you joke you would be if no catastrophe or obstacle got in your way. It is the person you crave to be despite challenges: "I'd be a nice person if I didn't have to deal with people."

It is the person you compare yourself to. You may compare your actions to what your ideal self would have done, especially when you're not proud of how you've handled something. It's thoughts like, "Ugh, I wish I'd been more patient, held my tongue, or thought it through better..."

Think of it as your "shoulda, coulda, woulda" persona. An aspirational self might come to you in the form of shoulds or shouldn'ts: "Crap, I should have said this instead" or "Darn, I shouldn't have done that."

Dr. Hardy says your identity comes from the standard you are firmly committed to. Think about listing your standards and the things you are committed to. For example:

- I am committed to walking every day. It's part of my identity. I identify as a walker. I am a walker.

- I don't just attend Toastmasters; I am committed to my growth and to the club's development. So, I say "I am a Toastmaster" rather than "I attend Toastmasters."

- I am committed to writing. I don't just do it sometimes; I have a standard that I expect of myself, which is to write daily. I am a writer.

- I am committed to honesty and set standards for myself. If the cashier misses scanning the stuff under the cart, I'll bring it to their attention. I am honest.

Consider what words you would list after the prompt "I am..." These words will help you reveal the narrative you have about yourself.

Your identity drives your conduct. The standards you set for yourself and the commitments you follow through on show up in your conduct, which people see and use to judge your character. If you do not intentionally craft your future identity, you have no target to aim for. You need an aspirational identity, a target or goal that helps you shape today's behaviour.

Your aspirational identity is your best self, but you aren't always there. We are not perfect. We are human, and as such, at times, we flounder, fail, or fumble. This is when we are judged: not at our best but how we typically show up. According to Dr. Hardy, our floor—the typical us, not the best us (our ceiling)—is what people base their descriptions of us on. To be a character driven leader, you must keep aiming for your ceiling.

The catch is we aren't this person, this aspirational identity, and will never be. It's a moving target. When we get close, we see how much more we could be and set our sights higher. We get clearer about what it means to be that person and map out a new path.

In the same way, we never reach a thriving or magnetic state. Occasionally, we'll slide into those states, but for a fleeting moment. We feel the breathtaking experience of awe, a wash of gratitude or joy envelops us, and then it's gone. The thriving and magnetic states are moving targets too. We get a glimpse of them, and then we see an even higher goal to attain, so we set our sights higher.

Creating Your Aspirational Identity

If you have not already drafted your aspirational identity, now is the time to begin. Your plan will help you get there, but you need to know where *there* is. In essence, you are creating a vision board for your soul!

Take out your journal and begin to create your future identity. Keep adding to and altering it, as your vision grows as you grow. Start with the values, strengths, and traits you want to hold onto that you identified when you embraced your essence. Add the things you want to grow, which you revealed as you pondered your potential.

Then consider these questions:

- Who do I want to be?

- What kind of a leader do I want to be remembered as?

- What kind of a leader do I want to be known as?

- What is the impact I want to have as a leader?

- What am I striving for in my leadership?

Develop a story about how you want to lead and live. Write about a day in your life a year from now. I have multiple versions of these in various journals. They all change a bit, but common themes run through them all, which give me insight into the person I have the potential to become.

Take time to complete the following sentence prompts imagining you already have the "perfect" life, career, and relationships:

- This is the kind of person I've become...

- These are the kinds of conversations I have...

- These are the kinds of things that are now happening...

A future-self visualization can also help. You'll find a link to one at kathyarcher.com/cdlextras.html. Once you have drafted your vision for your ideal self, it's time to create your plan for getting there.

Create Your Character Development Plan

I'S TIME TO create your plan to help you move from who you are to who you want to be. It's important to note that your plan can not stay in your head. You must write it down. And your plan must incorporate a system you can use daily—yes, daily. We want to ensure you have micro-moments throughout your days to increase awareness, time to learn, and active choices to cultivate your character.

A Ninety-Day Plan

We won't be creating a plan for an entire year. We work much better in sixty- or ninety-day cycles. Ninety days is about as long as our brains will take us, and it keeps the timeline short enough that we won't put off action until later. We know what projects and events are coming up at work. We can see what's on the horizon in our personal lives—kids' tournaments, family vacations, or moving homes. This gives us a better idea of what we can realistically accomplish in the next three months and what might be best to focus on.

You can set annual goals, and you should, but then break them down, creating short-term plans throughout the year. This allows you to try something out, to plan, practise, review, and revise. Shorter periods also allow for celebrating successes and course correction where needed.

A Practical Plan for Character Development

It is time to put together all of what you've learned so far and make it actionable. The goal is to move from an inventory of character traits, which you intend to emulate, to living them every day. Your plan will answer the following question: "How will I move from listing words about who I endeavour to be to actually living those words?"

Pull out your notes, lists, and journals. Look at what you discovered when you embraced your essence and pondered your potential. What is the gap between who you are and who you want to be? What's the gap between your ceiling and your floor? And how will you narrow that gap?

There is more to goal setting than just writing a sentence down. There are the four aspects of a goal that I highly recommend you include to ensure you develop your character:

1 You need to know the *target* you are aiming for.
2 You need to get clear on your *pathway* to that target.
3 You need a *measurement* to chart your progress.
4 You need a *timeline* for reviewing progress and redefining your target.

Your Target
Your goal is the target you are aiming for. Rather than goals about what you want to achieve, you'll be looking at what kind of person you want to become and the impact you want to have.

The idea is to rough out your goals. Draft two or three goals to help you achieve your vision. They don't need to be perfect, smart, or finalized. "Draft" is the important word here. You'll continue to refine them as you work on them. Just get something down on paper as a starting point.

You'll develop an overarching goal that is attached to character and then smaller goals to help you get there. It may help you to think of these smaller goals as things you want to feel, think, and act. For example:

- Overall target: *I have grown my leadership capacity.*

- Smaller target: *To read one book on leadership this quarter.*

- Feelings I'll create: *Curiosity, intrigue, confidence.*

- Action habit: *I will read five minutes each morning before work.*

- Mindset habit: *When I think I don't have enough time, I will remind myself that character development happens in micro-moments.*

I know it feels weird to plan how you want to feel. However, you've learned that feelings are an incredibly important part of character development. When you ask yourself what you want to accomplish as a goal or aim for that target, your feelings are the why, which reflects your purpose and your values. It's about your aspirational identity. Ask yourself why it matters so much to aim for being that type of person.

You may start by noticing what feelings you don't want to feel.

- You are tired of feeling stuck.

- You don't want to feel exhausted.

- You hate the constant feeling of overwhelm.

- You are fed up with the repetitiveness of the same old hamster wheel.

Then turn those around to consider how you do want to feel. As much as possible, create goals that are positive, such as:

- To feel more energetic

- To feel more at peace with myself

- To feel a deeper sense of connection with someone

- To feel more engaged in my work

Including feelings in your goals is critical for character development. Don't overlook this step. You'll want to craft your target statement in positive and future-focused language as if you've already done it. In the example above, it was "I have grown my leadership capacity." Here are more examples of reframing your statements to be positive and future-focused.

Negative	Positive
I want to stop dilly-dallying about decisions.	I am a decisive leader.
I want to stop ignoring the relationship component of leadership.	I balance tasks and relationships.
I want to stop getting caught up in crises.	I lead with a strategic focus.

Your Pathway

Now it's time to create your strategy or plan. What are the pathways to help you stay on track as you move toward your target? Think of this as your personal and professional learning curriculum. It isn't just one thing but multiple things you'll consider to help you stay on track. When creating your plan, ask yourself:

- What knowledge do I need to increase?

- What skills or strategies do I need to practise more?

- What feeling, thinking, and acting habits am I creating?

Consider what will aid in your development in terms of tools, resources, and support. In my mind, if you don't have a binder or a journal to write in, you aren't learning strategically. Remember, self-reflection is key for character development. These tools help you self-reflect.

Look at where you can get training for the skills you've identified:

- Take an in-person course
- Register for an online program
- Read a book on the subject
- Think beyond typical training opportunities

While your local college may have a course on spreadsheets, there may not be a college course for learning to inspire. Therefore, you may add to your book list, attend webinars, find a mentor or coach, or take training that will help you grow from the inside. We know that confidence is what you think you can do, so start looking at retraining how you think.

To help you stay on the right path, the six practices in the final section of this book will help you become the leader you desire to be. Don't skip that final section! It's all about habits. Habits of learning, being curious, moulding your mindset, jotting in your journal, and weaving in wellness. These habits will create your outcomes. These are the fundamental micro-steps that will help you achieve your goals and move closer to your aspirational identity.

These habit targets are the subset of goals to reach your main target. Ask yourself what habits you need to weed out and what new habits you need to grow.

- **What are your thinking habit targets?** What thoughts are you working on? What attitude do you need to cultivate? What mindset do you need to come back to on a regular basis?

- **What are your feeling habit targets?** What are the feelings you are aiming for and what feelings will you need to habitually cultivate to get there? How will you do that?

- **What are your action habit targets?** What things do you need to do daily to stay on the right path? What action habits will help you create a new way of thinking? What action habits will help you be more aware of your choice points so you can think before acting?

To become proficient at a skill, you need to practise it. By habitually practising the skill, you will know you can handle it when that skill is being called upon.

Your Measurement

What gets measured gets improved, but how will you measure your progress? You may be wondering how to measure goals that seem immeasurable. Here are three ways:

1 Measure the use of the tool.
2 Measure the habit you need to instil to help you reach your target.
3 Measure the milestones along the journey.

To measure the use of the tool, think about what you will use to help you reach your goal. Get clear on how you will use that tool. Then measure the usage of that tool. For example:

Target: Be better able to focus on important but not urgent work

Tool: Practising meditation

Measurement: Record how frequently you meditate

Target: Feel more confident in staff meetings

Tool: Journal to track and shift thoughts

Measurement: Record how often you journal your thoughts and when (pre-meeting, post-meeting?)

Target: Spend more time on strategic thinking

Tool: Going for a walk to get away from your desk

Measurement: Count the times each week you walk and are alone with your thoughts

The second way is to measure the habit you need to instill to help you reach your target. If your goal this year is better work-life balance, for example, habitually leaving work on time will provide more balance. You could track how often you leave work at five o'clock.

To feel more confident in staff meetings, you'll need to be more intentional before staff meetings. Choosing how you will respond instead of reacting to a trigger needs to become a habit before meetings. You could measure how often you preplan managing your emotions during meetings. Is it becoming a habit that you naturally do?

When you find yourself stuck on a problem, you've likely been trying to figure it out in a linear, analytical, or in-the-box way. Instead, you may need to think more freely, creatively, or strategically. When you schedule thinking time into your week, you'll be on your way to finding more time to think by creating that habit. Count the times you do it. Has it become a weekly habit yet?

You can also measure milestones along your journey to your goal. Completion of goals takes time and often involves many steps. However, we feel more engaged in our goals when we can see progress along the way. For example, a target of being more focused means you

- hit milestone 1 by getting a tool: You picked and installed the app you'll meditate with.

- hit milestone 2 when you use the tool: You started with two minutes per day, and a week later, you moved up to three minutes.

A target of feeling more confident means you

- hit milestone 1 when you found a journal or scribbler to note your thoughts.

- hit milestone 2 when you began habit forming. You journaled for at least five days in one week

A target to increase strategic thinking means you

- hit milestone 1 when you went for a walk to think, despite feeling guilty about all the work you were putting aside.

- hit milestone 2 when you told someone you were "going to think" and did not apologize or feel guilty about it.

Your Timeline

Dr. Piers Steel, a researcher at the University of Calgary, has uncovered a formula that addresses procrastination and helps to increase your motivation: procrastination or motivation equals expectancy times value over impulsivity times delay.

Expectancy is what you expect to happen. Expectancy includes how competent you feel you are to do what is required. *Value* is your belief in the worthiness of doing the thing. *Impulsivity* is your ability to resist urges, temptations, and distractions. *Delay* is how long the timeframe is for completing the task. The larger the delay, or timeframe, means the less motivated you are to get it done today. The farther away the due date is, the more we procrastinate.

So, keeping your timeline shorter for smaller tasks will motivate you to do them. Ask yourself what can be done this week. Coming up, we'll be talking about a weekly review. That's when you'll be setting these micro-targets.

Example of a Character Development Plan

I helped my client, Divya, develop her quarterly Character Development Plan. To help you develop your plan, let's look at what she came up with:

Target: Increased work-life balance

Pathway: Delegate more and reduce the number of working hours

Seems simple enough, right? If you have too much to do, give some of it away. We all know that it's not quite that simple, so I asked her what roadblocks might get in the way of that. Divya indicated she was worried about overwhelming her staff if she delegated more to them. If that's the case, she'll fail at her goal before she even starts. Even though Divya wants to reduce her hours and delegate more, her thoughts would get in the way, and she won't follow through.

Divya's assumption that her staff would be overwhelmed had become a habitual way of thinking. When we looked more closely at that perception, Divya realized there was some truth to it, but there was more to the story. After some coaching, Divya came up with these four realizations:

1 If Divya delegated more to her managers, it would help them grow, develop, and advance in their careers.

2 Divya also needed to teach her managers how to delegate to *their* teams. She realized she'd been role modelling an "It's easier to just do it yourself" style of leading.

3 At times it would too much for her managers and their teams if she delegated, which mean that was an issue for Divya to bring to upper management.

4 If Divya delegated more, she would get out of the weeds of micro-managing. Instead of doing the work of a line manager, delegating would enable Divya to move more into leadership functions.

To achieve her goal, Divya needed to not just look at the outcome she desired and the strategy to get there but at what mindset shifts she needed to make to believe it was possible. This is what she came up with:

Target: Increased work-life balance

Pathway: Delegate more and reduce the number of working hours

Mindset Shift: Delegating helps not just me but my managers and our team

Rather than goals about what you want to achieve, **you'll be looking at what kind of person you want to become and the impact you want to have.**

We then worked on operationalizing this goal into a daily habit that would lead to Divya achieving success. Divya realized there was no magical number of things she needed to delegate or even types of things. It was about being intentional about her workload and the process of delegation. She created a habit to help her proceed through the Infinite Leadership Loop (which you'll be learning to do shortly).

Pause: Grab her notebook with her running to-do list and sit down for three minutes.

Ponder: Make a few notes about a delegation choice point in her day.

Pivot: Consider if her thoughts helped her and her team get to where they needed to go, considering work-life balance, program goals, and staff developmental needs.

Proceed with her **people:** If she realized something needed delegating, she'd either do it or make a note to follow up on it.

Are you still unsure how to create your plan? Let's look at some more examples to help you.

Examples of Character Development Targets and Pathways

Aspirational Identity: I am a courageous leader. I am stronger, more assertive, and more confident. As I grew, I could feel myself doing tough things like addressing issues, setting boundaries, and being true to myself.

Target: I feel more competent and confident in my leadership role.

Pathway:
- Learn to manage my thoughts by reading and applying the concepts in *Mastering Confidence: Discover Your Leadership Potential by Awakening Your Inner Guidance System.*

- Learn more about leadership competencies by listening to podcasts on the topic.

- Practise public speaking by joining Toastmasters.

Measurement:

- I read *Mastering Confidence.*

- I can name three competencies that are important for me to develop.

- I gave three speeches at Toastmasters.

Aspirational Identity: I am a leader who is seen as being genuine, honest, and authentic.

Target: I lead with integrity.

Pathway:

- Gain a better understanding of what integrity is and what it would take for my employees to judge me as being in integrity.

- Review feedback on my performance appraisals to understand where my team is judging me as out of integrity.

- Have conversations with Cindy, Don, and Justin, whom I feel safe with, regarding their feedback.

- Journal about what I discovered about my reputation.

- Complete the values exercise to clarify my values and how they manifest at work and in my life.

- Complete the VIA Character Strengths profile.

- Create a habit of journaling about how in alignment I felt each day with my three core values; when I felt unaligned; and what actions, mindsets, or habits would bring me back in alignment.

Measurements:

- Feedback on my annual performance review indicates staff see me more positively.

- My own gut score on a ten-point Likert scale measuring how aligned I feel with my three core values.

A Likert scale is a survey tool that measures people's attitudes or opinions by asking them to rate statements on a multi-point scale—from 1 to 5, or 1 to 10—typically ranging from "strongly disagree" to "strongly agree."

Aspirational Identity: I feel courageous when I take aligned actions.

Target: I engage in difficult conversations rather than avoid them.

Pathway:

- Read Brené Brown's book *Daring Greatly*.

- Watch inspirational movies that showcase bravery, and journal lessons that you take from them.

- Keep a fear journal, noticing thoughts, physiological sensations, and emotions.

- Answer the following questions each day in my journal: What will I do today that is outside my comfort zone? Where do I plan to fail today?

Measurement: I will record failures. When I am failing more often, it means I am stepping outside my comfort zone and being brave. I will see the score increase gradually to a point I feel is helping me stretch but not snap.

Aspirational Identity: My actions align with my values. Even though that's hard sometimes, I still align with courage.

Target: I show up more honestly and authentically.

Pathway:

- Increase my self-awareness of who I am at my core by journaling each day about where I felt most myself.

- Journal about what I was doing and enjoying when I was a youth as that will help me remember who I am at my core.

- Complete the VIA Character Strengths profile.

- At my weekly review, journal about one of the following prompts: "If I was honest with myself...," "My truth is...," "My authentic self would...," or "The way I really want to deal with this is..."

Measurements:

- Is my list of authentic traits, strengths, and values growing?

- Does it feel aligned with my actions?

Now that you know how to develop your plan and you've begun drafting it, it's time to keep it front and centre with you every week via the mandatory weekly review.

The Mandatory Weekly Review

The key to character development is self-reflection; however, you need to pause to do that self-reflective work. The purpose of a weekly review is to intentionally pause and assess what you've done and who you've become and then recommit, course correct, or remove a goal as you plan for the upcoming week. If you wait until the ninety days are up, you may be way off course or have stopped heading down the path altogether, thus it's mandatory to do a weekly review.

Think of your weekly review as a micro-moment that shapes your character. Habitually using these micro-moments to review where you are on your journey toward your target means giving yourself more choice points to make you more successful. Being determined, even though adversity will always hit, is how you achieve your goals and become a strong leader.

The actions you take on the journey to achieving your goals make a difference. However, the hard part is consistently taking action. In truth, many of the steps you need to take to achieve your goals won't be easy or enjoyable. That is precisely why many people don't achieve their goals. They stop when it gets tough or they encounter a barrier.

Here is the thing though: you need those roadblocks! Not only does adversity strengthen you, but as the saying goes, "Adversity doesn't build character. It reveals it." The difficult parts are essential. By overcoming struggles, we learn, grow, and become better versions of ourselves. It is during challenges that we become better leaders. Getting through the trying segments of the journey is necessary for reaching the goal.

The habit of reflecting on these challenges with a growth mindset helps you turn that adversity or trauma into learning and character development. When you hit a roadblock, feel overwhelmed, or want to quit, your weekly review will help you reconnect to your aspirational identity. From that place, you'll have ideas of how to get over the hump. Reviewing your plan will remind you of what you can do when you feel overwhelmed, confused, apprehensive, or stuck.

The following steps provide a process for your weekly review of your goals and strategic plan:

The Framework for Your Weekly Review

Each week, set aside ten to thirty minutes to review your goals and the plan you have for achieving them. During this time, create the habit of doing the following.

Review your targets. You might want to rewrite them. Writing your goals down creates new pathways in your mind that activate the desire to achieve them. It keeps them alive and real. You don't have to write out all the steps, just the overarching goal. This step is all about creating the habit of tuning in to who you are becoming and making decisions from that place more often.

Visualize yourself achieving your goals. Close your eyes and imagine what it will be like when you reach your goal. Connect emotionally and viscerally to it. Feel the excitement, pride, and sense of accomplishment. Let your tummy get jumbly and your heart swell and your eyes water. Remember feelings are embodied, and feelings are fundamental for character development. Try to get to this place each week as you review your goals. It won't always happen, but the more you practise, the more you'll be able to drop into the feeling of that future self.

Review your progress. Where have you increased your knowledge or skills? What skills or strategies did you practise? How are you doing with your habits of feeling, thinking, and acting? Take time to consider what's working and what got in your way. Reflecting on these insights will help you course correct.

Review where you are on your plan. Remind yourself of the steps you identified in your Character Development Plan that you need to take to reach your aspirational identity. Are you still on the right path? Are there things you need to keep doing, stop doing, or do more or less of?

Visualize your next steps. Close your eyes again and see yourself navigating your steps for the upcoming week. As you do, notice challenges that may pop up and envision yourself overcoming them. As you see yourself moving toward your goal, notice what it takes for you to progress through the difficult times. It may be your determination, patience, or persistence.

Identify your focus for the coming week. As you review your plan each week, identify what you need to work on to keep moving toward your goals. Write that action down. Then schedule it in your day timer and commit to doing it. If it's a mindset shift, note how you will make use of your micro-moments to reset your mindset. For example, "This week, I will narrow the gap between where I am now and where I want to be by..."

I've also identified questions and journal prompts that you may want to add in during your weekly review, which you'll find at the back of the book in the appendix and more on my personal website.

The Quarterly Review

The quarterly review is much the same as the weekly review but pulls you into a larger view. This is when you look at your full ninety-day plan, assessing what you've done, who you've become, and where you are now on your path. Your quarterly review takes more time than your weekly review, but it can be done in micro-moments if you are struggling to find a chunk of time to do it in. Like in the weekly review, you'll want to do the following:

1 Review your targets.
2 Visualize yourself achieving your goals.
3 Review your progress.
4 Review where you are on your plan.
5 Visualize your next steps.
6 Identify your focus for the next quarter.

This is your opportunity to recommit to the person you are becoming. You may want to add to your aspirational identity or modify it. You may have realized a skill gap that leaves you feeling incompetent, and you'll want to add that to your list. You may also incorporate feedback you've received. That may be formal or simply checking in with others to see if they are feeling the difference.

Then plan your next quarter. Rewrite your targets and plans if necessary. This is about the constant ebb and flow of doing the inner work of the Infinite Leadership Loop so that you can create the character you desire.

I encourage my students to review the worksheets from the Training Library, which help them assess and measure their growth. One worksheet gets them to relist their values, how they define them, and then identify how they have been operationalizing their values for the last three months. Another sheet has them rate how effectively they have been using the Infinite Leadership Loop by scoring themselves on each point of the mobius. You will learn in the next section that pause counts twice. If they score lower on that, they know where to put their focus. A third worksheet reminds them that their conduct defines their character. They are asked to list the work they've done to "clean up" their conduct and make it consistent with the character traits they desire.

It's this level of self-reflection that helps you to get to your target, your aspirational identity. Pausing to ponder enables you to pivot and refocus on any area you want. Curiosity about how to do that will propel you into proceeding in the right direction with your people. (Now try saying that five times fast!)

The keys to remember as you rework your Character Development Plan are as follows:

- Self-reflection is the key to character development.

- Character development happens in micro-moments.

- Your decisions, especially your micro-decisions, shape your character.

- Habits are your superpowers.

- How you view things determines how you do things.

Let's look at my character development story. I decided to return to school for my degree, and it took eight years and countless hours of study time. I had to stay focused and set my parental guilt aside while my husband handled the kids' bedtimes and homework. The commitment required a ton of work to overcome inner saboteur voices that threatened to stop me dead in my tracks.

My plan helped me to focus on what was in front of me. My pathway was to attain my degree slowly and steadily: one course at a time. I had created in my mind a future identity for myself as a skilled, effective, and confident leader. I strategically planned which courses to take and in what order to coordinate with what was happening in life. I took a couple of semesters off to recharge. I kept my end goal in mind, managing my thoughts when doubt, fear, and hesitation crept in. My pathways were clear, knowing what chapter I was reading, what paper needed completing, what I needed to do that evening and perhaps the next. Both my long-term vision of my aspirational identity and the daily steps of the plan were crucial to my success.

The Final Step: The Feedback Loop

Let's review where we are with the steps for developing your character:

1 You've increased your awareness of how your character is developed.

2 You've gotten to know your true essence better, including your character strengths, values, ethics, and morals.

3 You've created a vision of your aspirational identity.

4 You've created your Character Development Plan to help you reach your aspirational identity.

Now it's time to move to step 5, which is to build a system of ongoing self-reflection, feedback, and practice, followed by more reflection, feedback, and practice.

The three steps covered in this chapter—embrace your essence, ponder your potential, and engage in endless growth—are accomplished through the constant ebb and flow of the Infinite Leadership Loop. Let's dive into the loop now.

PART THREE

THE FIVE STEPS FOR SHAPING YOUR MANAGEMENT STYLE

8

The Infinite
Leadership Loop

HE FINAL STEP in strengthening your character is to build a system of ongoing self-reflection, feedback, and practice. This step is all about the third character building question to engage in endless growth: "How am I developing now?"

Developing your strength of character is not a snap-your-fingers-and-be-done exercise. To always lead with your strength of character, you will be on this journey for the rest of your life. You must move endlessly around the Infinite Leadership Loop with curiosity. Constantly pausing, pondering, pivoting, and proceeding with a growth mindset will allow you to consciously create newer versions of yourself, knowing you'll never reach an end point.

Endless growth happens with the ebb and flow between outward engagement in life and turning inward for reflection. After a reflective pause, you reengage with your work and your people. Later, you'll take time once again to reflect. You'll notice some of what you did or the intentions you brought to work were successful, but others didn't produce your desired results or impact. Returning to the pausing, pondering, and pivoting of the Infinite Leadership Loop helps you iterate your thoughts, choose your feelings, and set new intentions. You can prepare how you want to act, how you will engage, and how you want to respond to potential triggers.

THE INFINITE LEADERSHIP LOOP

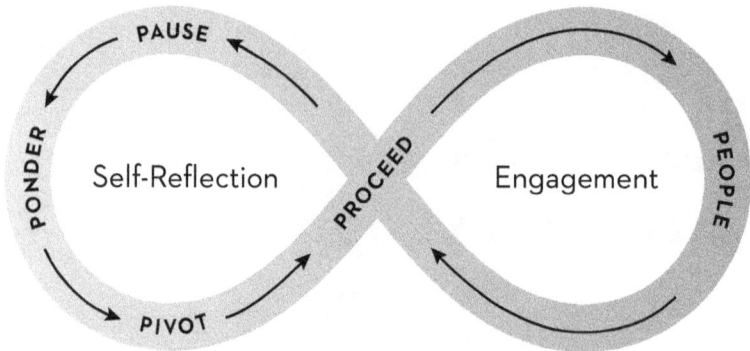

PAUSE

PONDER

Self-Reflection

PROCEED

Engagement

PEOPLE

PIVOT

Intentionality About Your Decision Points

You need to create a process, system, map, or guide to move into action. Instead of leaving it up to chance and simply hoping to become that person, you must identify the steps and daily actions to move toward living your list. Without the plan, you are leaving it up to chance, and chances are, you'll end up reacting when you wished you'd responded, regretting choices made out of anger, haste, fear, or despair, and not becoming the person you desire. Instead, you'll become a person caught up in everyone else's expectations, desires, and demands. You'll be a puppet and not a very happy puppet! If you want to be more in control of your leadership and life, make decisions aligned with the character you desire.

One of my clients, Jessica, was dreading an upcoming tough talk. Maybe you've been there too. These conversations make you squirm, want to gag, stir up intense emotions, and sometimes make you want to run away. I've been in many of these situations, and I felt I didn't handle it well because I wasn't my best self.

The thing is, it's our thoughts and perspective that make a tough conversation challenging. We *think* the conversation will be tough.

- We *think* there will be conflict, raised voices, resistance, or tears.

- We *think* others will be upset, dislike us, disagree, or cause more trouble.

- We *think* we will fall apart, lose it, be ineffective, railroaded, or dismissed.

- We *think* we can't handle these situations.

- We *think* our way into a tizzy!

Jessica had certainly done this. She could feel the anxiety in her body; she was concerned she'd be met with either defensiveness or combativeness when she addressed the issue, and Jessica worried she'd fall apart if that happened. She was losing sleep; she lay in bed rehearsing how bad it could go. She could feel

- her anxiety building,

- the ickiness inside of her growing, and

- the dread settling in to stay.

These kinds of body sensations and accompanying out-of-control thoughts cause us to believe we can't handle a tough situation, creating a lack of confidence to deal with it. I know that is not what you want! It certainly wasn't what Jessica wanted. Like Jessica, you, too, want the confidence to handle your job, team, and people. It's not only about tough talks—it's about all aspects of work—but let's be honest, the majority of your challenges are about your relationships with others and how you navigate conversations.

Leadership is tough. You'll always have tough conversations to deal with. To find a way to lead with your strength of character, you need a system that will help you calm your whirling thoughts, connect to your inner self, and take courageous and morally aligned steps.

If you want to feel more competent, capable, and sure of yourself in your relationships, you need to increase your self-confidence by learning to manage your thoughts and feel more aligned with who you are at your core. You need to see it's possible to become the person you aspire to be.

With their strength of character, leaders rely on inner wisdom that provides strength, insight, and stamina, not just to survive but to thrive. Successful and confident character driven leaders access that inner wisdom by consciously choosing to tune in to it.

The problem is we aren't taught to tune in to our inner wisdom. As new leaders, we learned about scheduling shifts, what forms need filling out, and when and how to do cover off. But we were not taught what to do when we were uncomfortable addressing a problem or how to deal with our emotions during a team meeting when everyone seems to hate us. When those feelings arose, many of us assumed there was something wrong with us. We weren't cut out for leadership, were doing something wrong, or alternately blamed it on the crappy staff we had. None of that was true, not completely.

What may be more accurate is that we have yet to learn how to communicate effectively as a leader, what to do with the voices in our head that doubt we can handle it, and what to do with our anger when a comment at a staff meeting triggers us. We need to learn how to access our inner wisdom.

Your doubt, fear, and hesitation are fuelled by thoughts. You can change those thoughts. When you change your thoughts, you see things from a different perspective, and it can help make you more confident and more aligned in any situation.

Your Inner Guidance System

As I taught in *Mastering Confidence: Discover Your Leadership Potential by Awakening Your Inner Guidance System*, your Inner Guidance

With their strength of character, **leaders rely on inner wisdom that provides strength, insight, and stamina, not just to survive but to thrive.**

System is your internal navigational structure. Think of your Inner Guidance System as your personal GPS or as a compass. Your Inner Guidance System points you in the right direction acting as your moral compass.

In our coaching session, Jessica took time to pause and reflect on how she was dealing with the staff and preparing for the conversation. She learned the steps of the Infinite Leadership Loop to help shift her thoughts and shake her dread. By the end of our call, Jessica felt surer of herself and her ability to navigate the conversation with more confidence.

I asked Jessica to ponder by talking about the thoughts, feelings, and body sensations she was experiencing when she thought of the impending talk. She was anxious about dealing with the conversation. In the past, she had armoured up and tried to push down her feelings as she headed into similar conversations. Often, she'd find herself dealing with the situation aggressively, which didn't feel right to her and didn't produce the best outcomes. Each time, she'd thought she could stuff down her emotions and deal with the issue matter-of-factly, but instead she spent the whole time worrying she might not get through it without falling apart. At times, she'd raise her voice, and her face would flush. Other times, she'd hear her voice waver as her stomach tightened. All of these felt like clear signs to her of how she'd failed.

Next, we tapped into Jessica's essence. She was a caring leader with a big heart. At the same time, she had high expectations for herself and the team. Jessica talked about being hopeful that the situation could be resolved. (Hope is high on her VIA Character Strengths profile.)

Being reminded of her strength of compassion helped her prepare and plan how to start the conversation, what to do when she felt herself tearing up, and how to respond with compassion to the employee's anger. It would still be an emotional conversation, a challenge for both of them. The difference was now Jessica knew she didn't have to shut off her emotions. She needed to be prepared to manage them.

I asked Jessica how her best self might handle a situation like this. Jessica spoke of being confident, fair, and in control of her emotions. Pondering her potential helped her tap into that inner wisdom.

When we take time to think strategically about the issue, we can get control of our thinking mind, plan for how we will manage our emotions, and strategize a way to address the situation, which is what Jessica did next.

Jessica started to pivot the way she was thinking when I asked her:

- How do you want to feel in this meeting?

- What type of leader do you want to be?

- What will help you feel that way and show up that way?

Jessica's curiosity kicked in as she tuned in to her essence and her potential.

- I want to feel confident.

- I want to be seen as fair.

- If I plan out what I want to say, take a break, and go for a little walk before the meeting, I'll feel more in control of my emotions and comfortable sharing the hard message I need to communicate.

By intentionally thinking through the Infinite Leadership Loop, Jessica began to plan for the conversation. She proceeded

- with more confidence

- in a way that felt more authentic and aligned with the type of leader she wants to be

- knowing she could have the impact she desires on her team member

Self-reflection is fundamental for character development. But it doesn't stop there. Character is built in relationships. Being intentional only gets you so far. To create the character you desire, you need to have the conversations and communicate your intentions and then do what you said you'd do. That's where integrity is created.

Every action is self-defining. Your conduct is contributing to your character. Being more conscious of how you want to be defined, described, or talked about means you need to engage in self-reflection and engage with the people around you. The more conscious you are of flowing back and forth between the two parts of developing your character, the more effective you will be at creating the character you desire. This is a commitment to a life-long journey of engaging in endless growth.

It's time to go through the Infinite Leadership Loop in more detail, exploring what each point means.

- **Pause:** Stop and turn inward.

- **Ponder:** Tune in to what is going on inside you, who you are, and who you are becoming.

- **Pivot:** Shift your thoughts, emotions, and intended behaviour.

- **Proceed:** Move forward with intention.

- **People:** Engage with those around you.

In the next chapter, we'll start with building in pauses.

9

Pause

NOTHING HAPPENS without a pause. If you don't pause, you never ponder and never intentionally grow your character. If you are like most leaders, you spend a lot of time on the go. We go from one meeting to the next with barely a moment in between! As a result, we feel we never have time to go to the bathroom, eat our lunch, or make a note to follow up on that last meeting. The problem is that it is hard to do the work of character development when you don't have time to pause, slow down, and tune in so you can be more intentional moving forward. Think of it like a mantra: pause and ponder.

When I talked to my client Heather about pauses, she said to me, "When would I find time to pause?" You'll never find the time if you look at it that way. And yet character driven leaders create time to think, ponder, and tune in. It's easy, though, to resist pausing, taking a break, or spending time in self-reflection when you're overloaded, overworked, and overwhelmed. We mistakenly believe that we don't have time to take a break. Pausing is essential to developing confidence, becoming a courageous leader, and making value-based decisions. So really, we can't afford not to.

Most of us are so stressed that we spend most of our time reacting to whatever shows up. Because of our stressed state, we can't think clearly, and we don't take time to choose how we want to respond, engage, or lead in that moment. Pausing allows us to move from reacting to responding.

When we pause, our brain and body begin to relax, allowing us to get out of stress mode, and we can think more clearly, which is what awakens our inner wisdom. Being more relaxed enables us to manage our thoughts, respond, and make conscious choices instead of reacting to every crisis that pops up.

Rather than being present, most of us have a ton of racing thoughts whirling in our heads. Those racing thoughts are usually about a future worry or past incident that we are still stewing about.

Pausing settles your racing thoughts. When you pause, you are not in the future or the past but in the present moment. It's here that you can tune in to your essence and your potential. When you mindfully tune in to those thoughts, feelings, and sensations, you will find the inner wisdom that helps to guide you forward in alignment with your authentic self.

Learning to make pauses a regular part of your routine takes time. You won't always remember to pause when necessary, so you must schedule them. Eventually, you may reach the point where a trigger reminds you to pause. That trigger could be when you're feeling lost, anxious, irritated, or off-balance. Those might be signals to go for a little walk, take a deep breath, or spend some time figuring out why you are so agitated. But often we ignore those triggers. We push them aside because we have too much work to do. So, for now, don't wait for the trigger; schedule the time to pause.

Pausing Allows for Character Development Work

When you decide you need to regroup before you make a decision, you might take a breath, step away from your computer, or talk it through with your boss. This break or pause allows you to ensure your values and beliefs, and those of the organization, align with your decision. When we create a habit that has us slow down before making a decision, we can become responsive instead of reactive.

Decisions create character, and there are a ton of decision points during our day. For example, each morning, I put creamer in my coffee. I certainly don't consciously decide to pour a tablespoon, or perhaps two, into my coffee each morning. But what if I did? Would I put it in if I thought about it and paused for a millisecond before I poured it in? I just did the math and realized that three to four cups of coffee times two tablespoons each equates to 160 calories and 20 grams of unhealthy fat per day. Ouch! Perhaps, given I've stopped consuming most other milk products, I might reconsider using coffee creamer. However, I continue to do it because I rarely give it any thought. But it is a choice I make every day. It's not a conscious choice, but it's a choice nonetheless.

Here's the thing: I don't think most of us realize that half of what we do, we don't have to do. Or that much of what happens *to* us could have been different if we had chosen a different path. Life happens *to* us when we are not intentionally making choices.

I am not suggesting that you start thinking about every single decision daily. I am suggesting you follow through on way more of the decisions you make. For the purpose of this book, I am especially pointing you to be more conscious about key decisions that relate to your character and leadership. The more intentional you are about your choices and decisions, the faster you develop the leadership character you desire. But you need to pause to make a mindful character driven decision.

Pausing Counts Twice

In the course My Training and Growth Annual Analysis inside the Training Library, students review their growth over the past year. They complete a worksheet to evaluate their effectiveness at using the Infinite Leadership Loop. Each part of the cycle gets a score, and they total up the sections to get a percentage. In this assessment, the pausing score counts twice. That's because if you do not pause, none

You can't wait for time to pause.
You need to make time for pausing!

of the rest is happening. If you're not slowing down and connecting to what's going on in your body, your mind, your soul, to what you're feeling and what thoughts you're having, you can't undertake these intentional shifts.

- You won't be growing yourself consciously.
- You won't be engaging with other people in a conscious manner.
- You won't be able to control your emotions.
- You won't have the composure you want.

Pausing, slowing down, stopping, and tuning in are the critical first steps, and they count twice. Get really good at pausing. If you notice that you're not getting to the other stages of the loop in a way that helps you become the leader you desire to be, it means you need to do more work on adding pauses to your day.

The Kinds of Pauses You Need to Take

Look at your day and decide how you can add these types of pauses:

- **Body Break:** A physical break to go to the bathroom, eat, or move your body.
- **Soul Break:** A mindful moment to take a few breaths, meditate, or sit in peace.
- **Mind Break:** A moment to let go of thinking about work and all of the challenges you're facing.
- **Self-Reflection:** A time for leaders to ask themselves:

  What am I feeling?
  What am I thinking?
  What's going on in my body?
  What just went on with that person?
  What just happened in that meeting?
  What will help me be my best self in this situation?

- **Thinking Time:** Time to review, strategize, and plan.

You won't always remember to pause, so you need to schedule pauses into your workday. You can't wait for time to pause. You need to make time for pausing! Creating breaks in your schedule will help you build a habit of pausing to do the inner work of character development. It is important to start by establishing a routine of stopping and pausing.

Pausing could start with mindfulness. Practising mindfulness can make you a better leader because mindfulness helps you to

- be decisive and make better decisions

- have stamina to endure through long days

- remain calm and be more relaxed during crises

- be composed and maintain your cool when triggered by a comment

- focus and concentrate instead of feeling frantic and scattered

- prioritize by using your judgment about where to put your attention

Instead of being stiff, bristly, and focused only on tasks and results, mindfulness helps you be a warm, caring, compassionate, and emotionally and socially intelligent leader. And let's be honest, that's who you are at your core! You are kind, caring, and passionate about your work. Sometimes, we just get caught up in the mess of the day, lose contact with that part of ourselves (as we are unmindful), and fall out of touch with the human side of our leadership capacity.

Mindfulness doesn't necessarily mean meditation. While that may be helpful, and I encourage you to try it, you don't have to meditate to practise mindfulness. Start by simply adding moments of mindfulness into your day. This morning, I ate my breakfast. That's it. I just ate my breakfast mindfully with

- no music playing
- no book in my hand

- no phone beside me
- no TV, YouTube, or training course video on

Your senses are wonderful ways of bringing you into the present so you can be mindful. You can practise tuning in to your senses even during a meeting, travelling, or watching TV. Become more aware of the sounds around you: the fan running, the sound of your breath, the tone of the speaker's voice. You could look for colours in the room, noticing the ochre in the poster on the wall or the indigo on a scarf. You might actually enjoy the taste of your coffee for a moment.

Mindfulness is simply being mindful of this moment, of whatever is happening around you. Too often, we let our thoughts pull us back to what has just happened and regurgitate what went wrong. Or we focus on the future, fretting and worrying about what will happen. To be mindful is to be in this moment, with whatever is happening right now—it's that simple!

You can also experiment with a more formal meditation practice. I meditate with a guided session from either the Calm or Balance meditation app daily. It didn't start out that way. I started with a one-minute meditation video on YouTube. A one-minute meditation was a choice I made about who I was becoming, a choice to start acting that way now. Character is developed in these micro-moments.

Strategies for Pausing

Schedule it. Block time off in your schedule or day timer for pausing. If you think you'll remember to do it, guess what? You won't. Schedule it in. Then treat it as an important appointment with yourself—one that you wouldn't dream of cancelling or rescheduling.

Start small. Begin with short, manageable intervals, like one to ten minutes daily. These micro-moments build the foundation for character development.

Use reminders. Use the alarms on your phone, computer, or watch or use visual cues like sticky notes to remind you when it's time to pause throughout your day.

Remove distractions. Turn off notifications and create a quiet space to engage fully in pausing.

Set boundaries. Communicate the importance of your uninterrupted pausing time to colleagues, team members, and family. This is where your moral courage comes in.

Use tools and techniques. Use practical tools like mindfulness apps or journaling prompts to facilitate pausing.

Integrate pausing into daily routines. Insert moments into existing routines like commutes, time before or after meetings, and breaks. Incorporate pause moments, like practising deep breathing while waiting for a meeting to start.

An easy way to remember to pause is to schedule these three essential appointments with yourself weekly:

1 **Schedule in time for self-care:** Time to nourish your mind, body, and soul.

2 **Schedule in time for self-reflection:** Time for cultivating inner wisdom and clarity.

3 **Schedule in time for self-improvement:** Time for investing in your development.

Your body and your team will thank you!

10

Ponder

P ONDERING OR engaging in self-reflection is where the magic of character development happens. When you engage in self-reflection, you tune into your essence and create time and space to cultivate the identity you desire for the future. Pondering lets you decide the type of leader you want to become and figure out how to be that leader. Engaging in endless growth means you'll learn to be responsive, increase your emotional intelligence, maintain your composure, and make character driven decisions about how to interact with others, behave, and communicate. Pondering is also the stage of the loop when you return to the three character development questions:

1 Embrace your essence: Who am I?

2 Ponder your potential: Who am I becoming?

3 Engage in endless growth: How am I developing that now?

As a leader in a nonprofit, you know all too well how relentless things are. You've barely got time to breathe between calls, messages, and knocks at your door; you are just reacting to whatever pops up. However, when we ponder, we slow down enough to be responsive instead of reactive. Pondering allows us to explore what is happening in our minds and bodies and what is causing us to behave in certain ways. This allows us to make conscious choices about our behaviour.

When we fail to ponder consciously, we simply get stuck in the same thought patterns. Your thoughts may take over if you don't slow down to widen the gap between an incident and your behaviour. Instead of processing what is happening, you'll rehash the events and recycle the same emotions. Over and over again, the same patterns will appear in your mind, resulting in the same pattern of behaviour.

Pondering lets us make sense of what's happening in and around us and improves our decision-making. In pondering, we look at our thoughts, feelings, and body sensations as information that can guide us to possible change. A key influence on our behaviour is our emotions. Pondering allows us to manage our emotions better. But it starts with what we think about what is happening and its meaning.

What Does Pondering Mean?

1. Thoughts

An incident happens at work, and we simply react, right? Actually, after the incident but before our reaction is a *thought*. There is a minuscule moment in which much transpires inside your mind and body. You want to get a handle on this moment to develop your character. Too often, our thoughts are not conscious. Pausing and tuning in to your thoughts, you may realize you are thinking:

- They don't care.
- I can't handle this.
- They don't trust me.
- What a waste of time.

We want to drill deeper into that thought in the pondering step and see what's happening there. That thought plays a huge role in how you feel. Slowing down widens the gap between the stimulus and the subsequent feeling. With open curiosity, you want to detect what thought was there between the event and the emotional reaction. That way, you can change your thoughts and thus manage your emotional response.

2. Feelings

As we reflect on our emotions and feelings, we can better understand and manage them, thus increasing our emotional intelligence. Our emotional stability gives us the ability to respond with integrity, patience, compassion, humility, or any other trait you want to develop or strengthen as you build your aspirational identity.

Just because you experience an emotion does not mean you need to express that emotion. You get to control how you express what you feel rather than your emotions controlling you. To increase your emotional intelligence, you'll use this stage of pondering to become aware of your emotions, name them, and then choose how you want to express them. Go back to the Feelings Wheel (feelingswheel.com) to find more granularity and specificity for your feelings.

For example, anger is an emotion that tells you something is in the way. This clue can help you get curious about what might be blocking you from something. When you feel attacked, it's because you feel like someone is taking something from you. What do you feel is being taken from you? Your credibility? Your job? Your sense of balance?

When pondering, we call in our curiosity to help us look both backwards and forward, and we identify what emotions we want to feel. Consider, for example, how you want to feel at the end of a staff meeting: confident, appreciated, grateful. You can map out what thoughts would create those feelings, what you'd need to do, how you'd need to act, and what impact you'd want to have on others to get to that point.

3. Body Sensations

Our bodies speak to us through our body sensations. What is happening in your body strongly indicates your thoughts and feelings. In fact, we feel before we think. The quicker you can tune into your body sensations, the quicker you can get a hold of your thoughts.

Keep this list of body sensations handy so you can refer to it, build on it, and note what emotions you experience when these sensations happen in your body. Your body sensations may be the first clue you have that your thoughts are unaligned with your aspirational identity.

- You soften.
- Your face or ears turn red.
- Your stomach tightens or knots up.
- Your heart races.
- You tense up.
- You lean in.
- You tear up.
- You have sweaty palms or armpits.
- Your body heats up.
- You have a headache.
- You feel a sense of inner calm or peace.
- Your throat tightens.
- You see red.
- You feel cold.
- Your body vibrates.
- You get butterflies in your stomach.
- Your heart swells or aches.
- Your fists clench.

You can grab a copy of these body sensations on the book's resource page at kathyarcher.com/cdlextras.html.

Looking back on a conversation, you may remember a change in your breathing pattern. Shallow breaths or breath-holding moments may have indicated your inner turmoil and instinctual response to stress. Maybe you were sweaty. That clamminess may have been your body's attempt to regulate temperature in the face of heightened stress levels. When your face begins to heat up, and you feel the wash of shame coming over you, you can ask yourself what you might be ashamed of or embarrassed by. These are all helpful clues to discover what you are thinking and feeling.

Emotions are felt in different parts of our bodies in different ways. Our chests can feel the warm glow of love or the dark tightening of anger. The same spots of our bodies can experience different feelings. Tuning in to your body sensations provides physical clues to your emotions in the moment. The sensation is linked to the emotion. These questions can help you tune in to your body sensations:

- Where am I feeling this in my body?
- How intense is the sensation?
- Is there a temperature change in my body?
- Is there a colour connected with the sensation?
- Am I feeling like I am opening up or tightening?

4. What's Happening Around You

You are also pondering what's going on around you. If someone snapped at you and your reaction was to snap back, you may get curious about what caused them to be harsh.

- Is something happening in their personal life?
- Could work be a bit too much for them at this time?
- What happened before the comment?
- What role might I have played in their reaction?

Pondering isn't all about you. It's also about the world around you and your interactions with it. Character is built in relationships. Your organization goes through cycles of events, busy times, and shifts in sector-related expectations. This plays a role in what's going on for you and others, and it will impact how you want to show up.

5. *Your Identity and Impact*

Finally, you are pondering your current and aspirational identities. Sometimes, you are reflecting on something that happened, but just as often it should be proactive. Included here could be goal setting and review, verifying your values, or deciding how you want to show up at an upcoming event. Getting clear on your aspirational identity and the impact you want to have on others is crucial to character development.

Self-awareness is the foundation of pondering. But for what reason? Why do all of this thinking? The reason is to develop your character. Our behaviour communicates a lot about us to others, and to have our desired impact, we must maintain composure and emotional control. Pondering enables us to become emotionally intelligent leaders so we can be character driven leaders.

When you maintain composure in challenging situations, you demonstrate resilience, emotional intelligence, and self-control— qualities essential for effective leadership. Composure allows you to make decisions calmly and thoughtfully, even under pressure, which fosters trust and confidence among your team members. To get this outcome, you must be intentional.

Pondering is intentional thinking, reflecting, and contemplating. The problem is that much of our thinking is unconscious. Something happens. It can be anything, big or small, such as:

- You receive an email.
- Someone says something.
- You observed a raised eyebrow or a shrug.
- You noticed an inflection in someone's voice.

You have thought about what happened, and you unconsciously attach meaning to that event. Your body reacts physiologically, creating a body sensation. You experience an emotion or feeling such as bitter, insecure, or overwhelmed. In a nanosecond, this chain of events causes us to do or not do something. We send a terse email, snap at our admin, shut our door a little harder than necessary, or

Pondering lets us make sense of what's happening in and around us and improves our decision-making.

choose to overlook someone's poor conduct one more time. This behaviour can be an unconscious reaction or a conscious response. The choice is ours. Self-reflection allows us to slow down and choose a response that is aligned with our aspirational identity, cultivating our desired character.

Reacting could look something like this:

Antecedent	**An event happens.**
	An email comes to your inbox.
Thought	**You have a thought about that event and attach meaning to it.**
	"That was rude," "I don't want to deal with this," "Oh, here we go again!"
Body sensation	**Rather than seeing sensations as clues, they are irritants.**
	"No wonder my shoulders are so tense. This person is driving me nuts!"
Feeling	**You experience emotions.**
	Frustration, anxiety, irritation
Behaviour	**You react.**
	You roll your eyes, or you shoot back an insensitive email.

Responding looks a little different.

Antecedent	**An event happens.**
	An email comes to your inbox.
Thought	**You have a thought about that event and note the meaning you've attached to it.**
	"That was rude," "I don't want to deal with this," "Oh, I'm in this thought loop again."
Body sensation	**You notice with curiosity what is happening in your body.**
	Tension in your shoulders is a sign that you have too much on your shoulders and a reminder to assess what you are taking on.
Feeling	**You experience emotions.**
	Frustration, anxiety, irritation
Pause	**You choose to tune in to your experience.**

At this point, you ask yourself, "What are my thoughts, feelings, and body sensations? What do they tell me?" Maybe you realize you need to reflect before you do something. You grab your notebook with the sticky note on the front cover with these three questions:

- Embrace your essence: Who am I?

- Ponder your potential: Who am I becoming?

- Engage in endless growth: How am I developing now?

You might write in your notebook:

I'm a leader who loves to connect with others. Love and kindness are high on my VIA Character Strengths profile. When I'm not at my best, sometimes I forget to embrace that part of myself. I get too busy and lose contact with others, just whacking moles trying to stay caught up. I'm becoming a calmer and more responsive character driven leader. To do that, I may need to get up and walk around the block before I respond to that email.

On your walk, you pull up the Feelings Wheel on your phone. You sit down on the curb for a second and look it over. As you do, your eyes land on "exasperation." "That's it," you think. "Nailed it. I'm exasperated. I feel like I will never get through to this person."

"Wait a minute," you think, "that's also hopelessness. Eeek." You know that hope is a trait needed in leadership. You have also done some work on cultivating hope, and you know that you need to do pathways thinking. You need to devise not only one plan to work through things, but to instill hope that this employee can figure things out, you need to communicate that together, you'll work through plans A, B, and C to help them get there. Feeling a bit of excitement, you get up and head back to the office, thinking about several strategies that might help.

Behaviour	You respond.
	You send an email back that is kind, caring, and hopeful: "You continue to struggle with this, and I can imagine that's hard for you. Let's get together and talk about several strategies to tackle this, as I know you'd like to put it behind you and focus on the work you love to do!"

Slowing down to think your behaviour through kept you in emotional control, allowed you to lead with your strength of character, and had a much more positive impact on the employee.

Self-reflection helped with self-regulation and character development.

Pondering the Settings

A key component of reflecting and choosing how you will show up is about turning up or down the dials on parts of yourself. I often think about the equipment on stage for a concert: a mixer has many knobs on it. Think of those knobs as your traits, values, strengths, and so on. Sometimes, you need to turn up compassion; other times, you must turn it down. You may nudge boldness to a 2, courage to a 6, and patience all the way up to a 9. But in a different situation with a different person, you may turn up optimism and hope and dial down your humour. When you come home at the end of the day, and continue to choose how you show up consciously, you'll again need to be aware of which levels are on high and which could slide down. Instead of shutting off your emotions, you choose how to show up in different settings.

A quote I often share with clients to help them understand this is from the writer Anne Lamott: "You can point with the sword of truth rather than cut." Just because I'm honest doesn't mean I need to be utterly and bluntly honest all the time. There are ways of being honest in a more gentle but still truthful way at times.

Another way to think of self-regulation is like a stoplight.

- Red means stop: Control your impulses or emotions.

- Yellow reminds us to use caution: A measured response is needed.

- Green is go-ahead: It's safe to express your emotions more fully.

Being more self-aware helps you dial into the parts of you that you want to express in any given moment to have the impact you desire.

The Envision Model

When we ponder what's happening, you'll notice everything has energy. There is an intensity, a vibration, a beat to everything happening. As you develop your character, you'll realize that you have more control over that energy than you thought. When we think, we often *envision* something in our mind's eye. We see the person who did or will do something to us. Far too often, we visualize ourselves fumbling and falling apart again and again. There is *energy* behind that vision, either positive or negative. It feels good or bad. The energy has a speed: it can pick up speed, slow down, vibrate, radiate, or swell. The energy also has a mood, vibe, feeling, or essence. For example, it can be draining, disturbing, dull, hot, painful, intense, warm, or cozy.

All of this is creating the *emotion* we experience. Emotions are energy in motion. That emotion creates the *experience* we have. Your experience is your emotion expressed.

Think of a time when you've been mad at your partner or someone close. Something happened, but you didn't get to deal with it then. As the day progressed, your agitation built. Your thoughts swirled. You started to envision how the conversation would go when you got home. Instead of being agitated, you became angry. You had everything planned: what to say and how they will respond. You rehearsed the conversation in your mind a million times. And you could feel the energy building as the conversation neared. When you saw them, you spewed your words way more aggressively than you would have in the morning. It was because you built energy and emotion as you envisioned a certain experience.

I want you to learn to become aware of and use your choice points along the steps of this envisioning process. At any point in time, you can choose to envision it differently, thus creating different energy, emotions, and subsequent experience.

A word of caution: many women I talk to ponder with their partners or friends. I wholeheartedly believe this can be effective if you pay attention to confidentiality and to the energy you are building.

ENVISION MODEL

CHOICE POINTS

You can make a conscious choice based
on who you are and who you are becoming

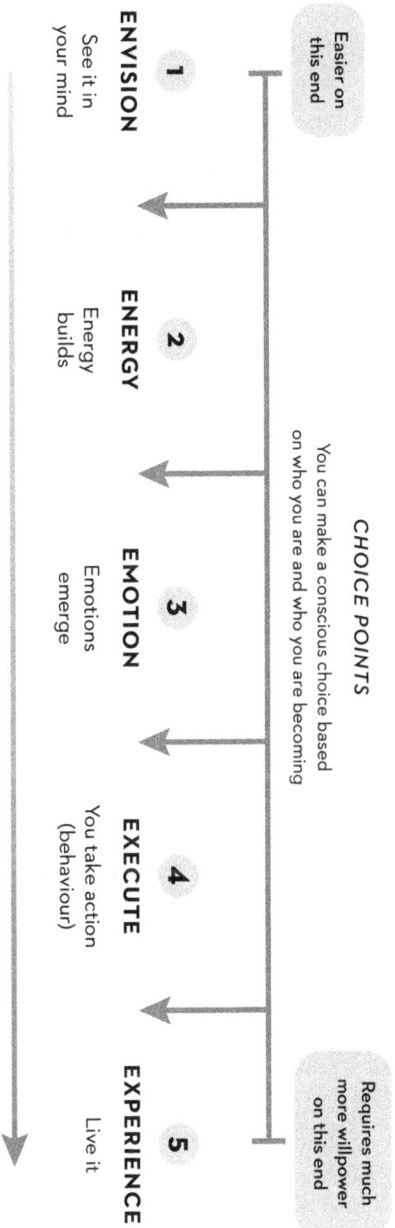

**Easier on
this end**

1
ENVISION
See it in
your mind

2
ENERGY
Energy
builds

3
EMOTION
Emotions
emerge

4
EXECUTE
You take action
(behaviour)

5
EXPERIENCE
Live it

**Requires much
more willpower
on this end**

ENERGY BUILDS

At this point, the
energy has built and
the urge is strong

The more frequently
you PAUSE, the sooner
you can create the
experience you desire

Is it the energy and emotions you desire or not so much? Is it building energy to help you become more aligned with your aspirational identity? Or is it spiralling into negativity?

Pay attention to the language you use with your partner. Remember my story of complaining about my employees to my husband? It was very much victim language: everything was being done to me. My negative energy was building. I was getting more worked up, adamant that I was right and it was their fault. The conversation wasn't helping me be my best self.

If I had been more aware of my words and then journaled that language later to practise new ways of thinking and expressing myself, I could have envisioned something more positive. I then could have practised that new mindset, with different energy, with my husband in future conversations. That would have resulted in a different experience.

The key to developing your character is self-reflection; it helps you learn to manage your thoughts. What you think, your opinions, and the meaning you attach to events impacts your vision of how everything will turn out. Pondering allows you to choose better thoughts that can guide you energetically to be your best self and develop your desired character traits.

Perhaps you feel that your boss is attacking you, and you feel backed into a corner. If you keep envisioning that, your reaction might be to get angry and come out fighting. Instead, by changing your envisioning perspective, your subsequent thoughts, feelings, and experience can be different.

With developed emotional intelligence, you might notice the following:

> I'm feeling attacked and notice my body getting into fight-or-flight mode. I remember reading somewhere that when I feel attacked, it means I feel like something is being taken away from me. What might I be afraid is being taken away, or what do I feel I am at risk of losing? I hate failure. I'm also worried the project is not going great. Maybe my boss is trying to say more about the project and

not me. He's probably also afraid we might fail if we don't get it back on track! We are actually on the same side. I sure as heck don't want this project to fail either. What strengths and traits can I bring to this project and to this conversation with my boss that might have the most positive impact?

Self-awareness increases anytime you can pause and tune in. It allows you to notice emotions and feelings, identify values, become aware of judgments and opinions, and acknowledge your behaviour. All of this will help to increase your emotional intelligence, which is critical to leading a team well, doing the fulfilling work you are meant to do, and doing it in a way that feels aligned with you.

Working on this first step of bringing awareness to your emotions and feelings can be challenging. It's not something that comes naturally to us. At first, it may feel strange and awkward. However, by doing this work, you will automatically become more aware of what's happening inside you, allowing you to regain control and manage your feelings and responses to people and events. Remember that it takes time, so be patient with yourself. The effort and commitment will be worth it.

Thoughts to Feelings to Behaviours

Here are some examples of feelings that may be connected to your thoughts. You can use this list and add to it to help you get curious as you ponder what is going on for you. This helps you increase your emotional vocabulary, which is essential for emotional intelligence.

Thoughts	Feelings
They don't respect me.	insulted, bitter, infuriated, indignant, incapable
They are difficult to deal with.	anxious, distressed, fearful, timid, shaky, wary
They won't take me seriously.	annoyed, frustrated, inferior, provoked, irked
They won't even listen to me.	enraged, incapable, useless, skeptical, pessimistic
They think I'm unskilled or lack experience.	inferior, beaten down, panicked
I don't trust them.	wary, cool, doubtful, reserved
I don't know if I can handle it.	anxious, panicky, cowardly, tense, uneasy, miserable
They're a bully.	terrified, apprehensive, dread, mistrusting

It's hard to learn to increase your emotional intelligence in a charged moment. You must practise the skill first by looking back at what has happened and reflecting on it. Increased awareness of what happened between the event and your reaction to it requires intentional thinking and slowing down the events so you can notice things you didn't see at the time.

To learn to manage your expression of your emotions in the moment, you must create a routine of rewinding events and looking back to see what caused you to react in the first place. You must build in time to pause and ponder. Self-reflection is key to developing your character.

The best way to get the slow-motion replay effect is to write down what happened. When you set aside a few minutes to jot in your journal and let your thoughts and emotions flow on paper, you'll see more of what is there. It is critical to do this writing without judgment. You must let your pen just flow. The point is to see what you may have missed, got hooked by, or overreacted to.

Understanding and often changing our story are critical. The story you told yourself resulted in the feeling that caused you to say or do something you may regret. I use the word "story" for a reason. While we like to think of it as the truth, it's only our version of the truth. It is the story we make up based on our beliefs, values, past experiences, and more. It's our perspective. When we start to change that story or shift our perspective, we move into the pivot stage of the Infinite Leadership Loop.

11

Pivot

PIVOTING IS TURNING. We are turning to new ways of thinking and allowing our character to develop as we want. Pivoting is shifting how we see a person, problem, or project. It is changing our perspective. But a mental shift can do more than just shift our thoughts. Changing our perspective helps us to choose alternate responses, change how we engage with others, and sometimes take different actions. Pivoting actually happens in the pondering stage, too, but it's helpful to see it as distinct. If you don't feel a pivot of perspective and still feel unaligned, go back to pondering.

As you cultivate your leadership character, the ability to pivot is not merely a strategy; it's a fundamental skill that empowers you to navigate complexities with awareness, insight, and choice. Leadership will continue to present you with experiences, but only you can decide what they mean to you. We ascribe meaning to events through our values, beliefs, morals, and every experience we've had in life. We label events with our assumptions, opinions, and perspectives.

Pivoting, however, is not reserved for moments of crisis or change; it is a continuous process rooted in how we perceive and interpret our experiences. It creates psychological flexibility. Psychological flexibility, as described by Dr. Hardy in *Personality Isn't*

Permanent, is "the skill of being fluid and adaptive, holding your emotions loosely, and moving towards your chosen goals or values. You need psychological flexibility to reframe your past and imagine a future self. The more flexible you become, the less you'll be overwhelmed or stopped by emotions. Instead, you'll embrace and learn from them."

Pivoting isn't a reactive physical manoeuvre but a mental and emotional shift that allows leaders to navigate challenges with resilience, adaptability, and psychological flexibility. Through deliberate reflection, pivoting allows us to cultivate a different, more aligned mindset. At its core, pivoting is about embracing the multitude of perspectives within us and recognizing that our current perceptions shape our reality.

Imagine a leader paralyzed by self-doubt, convinced of their inadequacy and unworthiness. Such entrenched beliefs erode confidence and impede progress, trapping individuals in a cycle of self-sabotage, perpetual imposter syndrome, and survival mode. To break free from this pattern, we must cultivate awareness of our thought patterns and challenge ingrained narratives that no longer serve us.

Our perceptions need not be rigid. Each person, problem, or project allows us to change the meaning we've attached to them, shaping a new narrative about them. That pivot of perspective can significantly shape our character and enhance leadership effectiveness.

Consider a leader confronted with adversity: do they perceive it as an insurmountable obstacle or a chance to demonstrate resilience and resourcefulness? By consciously reframing their interpretation, they can pivot from a stance of victimhood to one of empowerment, reclaiming agency over their narrative and inspiring others to do the same.

We often fall into the trap of linear thinking, believing that events dictate predetermined outcomes—if *X* happens, then *Y* will happen.

- If John is late again, it means he's not loyal to the team.

- When Tina and Cindy work together, you know the paperwork won't get done.

However, true leadership lies in the realization that we have the agency to rewrite this equation—to pivot from a fixed mindset to one of limitless possibilities.

Perspectives Are...

As a leader, you will experience many circumstances, situations, and events, but only you can decide what those circumstances, situations, and events mean to you. When we take a perspective on an issue, we have a belief, assumption, or expectation about it.

- **Beliefs:** I believe I have too many things to do.

- **Assumptions:** I assume that if I tried to change things, I would get resistance.

- **Expectations:** I expect I'll never get to take a break.

- **Opinions:** They are so lazy.

- **Judgments:** They are a difficult employee.

- **Filters:** My team doesn't seem motivated enough to meet our goals.

- **Perceptions:** I don't have what it takes to be a next-level leader.

- **Stories and narratives:** Seeing so many worthy causes always struggling to make ends meet is frustrating. This sector will never change!

As Lisa Feldman Barrett writes in her book *How Emotions Are Made*, "You feel what your brain believes. Affect primarily comes from prediction." Our perspectives are our predictions, and we are creating our own outcomes.

We tend to limit what is possible by what we believe is true. If we see something as hopeless, it is. We tend to gather evidence that confirms this. It is a powerful filter that lets us only see certain things. The thoughts we have can turn into unconscious patterns in our minds. For example:

- **Judging:** He's wrong. That's stupid. She looks foolish.

- **Incessant worrying:** What if this happens? What if that happens? How will I deal with them?

- **Comparing:** I'm not _____ enough. I will never be able to... If only I could do it like her.

- **All-or-nothing thinking:** It's either this or that. If she won't do this, then I don't need her help! If it can't be done this way, there is no point in doing it.

- **Absolutes:** It has to be this way. I must do it. He has to go.

- **Victim thinking:** Why is everyone out to get me? Why can't things ever work out? We are always the last program supported.

- **Labelling:** I'm such a loser. He's just a jerk. She's cold.

These patterns of thinking become mindsets in which we get stuck. They narrow and close our perspectives. This means your mind is set at one point. Rather than seeing the event, such as the triggering comment or the message in the email, through multiple lenses, you're stuck in one view and one view only, thinking "It must be like this."

Why Do We Need to Pivot Our Perspective?

Our perspective is only our view at this moment from this vantage point. These thoughts are not absolute truths. They are beliefs, values, and attitudes you created unconsciously throughout your life. And while they may have gotten you to where you are, they may not get you to the vision you've created for yourself. The vision you have of yourself is some version of a strong, confident, and morally aligned woman. But sometimes we are off. And if our perspectives or perceptions are off, we don't get the outcome we desire.

In *A Course in Miracles* by Helen Schucman, the reader is reminded that "[you] respond to what you perceive, and as you perceive so shall you behave... You cannot behave appropriate[ly] unless you perceive correctly." It's an important reminder that if we lead with our strength of character, we must ensure our perceptions align with who we are becoming.

When you pause and ponder, you can look at your thoughts, perceptions, and perspectives objectively and see if they align with who you desire to be. This creates a choice point for deciding if these thoughts and thinking patterns still serve you. Shifting your perspective puts you back in the driver's seat of your emotions, giving you agency in how you subsequently handle and respond to everything leadership throws at you.

We see situations, people, and challenges from different vantage points that can change daily, depending on a wide array of things, including how well we slept the night before to an email we just opened. In the same fashion, we see situations, people, and challenges much differently than a co-worker, boss, or subordinate does. It's important to recognize that there are many different perspectives that we, or anyone else, can have.

The challenge arises when we aren't open to how others see things. Equally challenging is when we resist changing the way we see it. Most of us have tunnel vision. We want to see it only our way. We think our way is the best, the right, or the only way.

Truthfully, though, our view is only one view of everything. No two people have the same view of anything. Our outlook can change dramatically from one day to the next or in a split second. It all depends on what we are thinking. Pivoting requires us to change our thoughts.

How to Shift Perspectives

The truth that there are multiple perspectives to how we tackle leadership can help you be a more confident and effective leader. The first two steps of the Infinite Leadership Loop have helped you turn unconscious thoughts into conscious thoughts.

Leadership will
continue to present you
with experiences, but
**only you can decide
what they mean to you.**

Pivot is what to do with what you discover as you spend some time reflecting. In essence, pondering and pivoting happen together. We separate them to make the point that for the pondering to be truly successful, there needs to be a pivot in your thinking. It may be affirming that you are on the right path. That's a pivot in that you've decided you don't need to do anything when, at first, you may have thought you did.

We are usually unaware of what is going on inside us. Because we have not noticed what's happening inside, we also don't realize how our feelings and thoughts impact our confidence levels, our ability to manage our emotions, or how stuck we are in a particular perspective.

Be wary of looping thoughts. Repetitive looping thoughts, such as "I can't handle this," allow the idea to become an ingrained belief. Becoming aware that we've had the same thought ten times in the last three minutes makes examining the idea more carefully possible.

Conscious thoughts will help you gain insights. When we become more mindful of the fact that we repeatedly have a thought, we can inspect it. Is it true? Maybe not. Or maybe it is partially correct.

You can then ask yourself what parts are true. For example, "It is true that I can't handle it all alone." This new understanding helps us realize that we may need to learn something new, ask for help, or try a different approach.

Awareness helps to shift our thinking and allows us to pivot our perspectives. This change in thinking allows us to see the problem and ourselves differently. Rather than the repetitive thought of "I can't," we can pivot to "With help, I can handle this." Suddenly, the load seems a little lighter and our confidence increases.

Steps to Pivot Your Thinking

Pivoting allows you to get from where you are now, which is often stuck, to where you want to be. Think of it as an intersection.

- **Pause** when you get there
- Tune in and **ponder** for a moment.
- **Pivot** by looking at the direction you are currently going. Consider the alternatives. Which road ahead of me will get me to the future vision I desire?

These steps will help you consciously turn your thinking.

1. Become Aware of Your Thoughts

Pausing and pondering have helped you become aware of your thoughts. Now write them down. Journaling allows us to review our thoughts and see them more objectively. You won't have to journal all the time, but practising this step is extremely helpful.

2. Evaluate the Thoughts

To change your thinking, you'll need to examine your thoughts consciously. Here are some questions to ask yourself to help you do this:

- Even if this thought was once true, is it still true?
- Is this thinking getting me to where I want to be?
- How else could I look at this problem, person, or project?
- What is in my way of seeing this differently?
- What would move me forward on this?
- Where or who could I ask for help?
- Which of my strengths would help me navigate this challenge easier?

Brené Brown encourages us to reframe how we see our current situation by starting our sentences with "The story I tell myself is..."

3. Create New or Updated Versions of the Thoughts

Now, rewrite your thoughts in a way that serves you. This is where you plan, prepare, and practise for future conversations.

- Plan the outcome you want. How do you want that person to feel when they leave the conversation? What impact do you want this conversation to have on your relationship with them? How do you want to feel when you finish the conversation?

- Consider what mood, emotions, and energy you need to bring into the conversation to achieve that outcome. Plan what you'll say, what behaviours you need to consider, and how to manage your emotions when triggered.

- Plan for the action or behaviour change you want, and plan how you will create the energy and mood to effect that change.

Let me tell you how pivoting worked for Emma. Emma had someone on her team who was perpetually late with her paperwork. It didn't matter how often Emma talked to this person; it never seemed to change.

When I was coaching Emma, I reminded her she *could* continue having the same supervision discussions with this team member and address the late paperwork. That approach would likely cause friction, and the employee would continue feeling frustrated, perhaps stupid, or unsupported. The team member sees Emma as nagging her but doing nothing to help her, possibly even garnering Emma the reputation of being a micro-manager, control freak, or perfectionist.

Unpacking things through coaching, Emma saw that in her mind, there was a right way to do things: handing things in on time. As a result, Emma also believed that this employee is doing things the wrong way: submitting items late. Emma's thinking and subsequent reactions to late paperwork left the employee only able to defend themself, making excuses about why they weren't measuring up and offering promises they would never keep. So, the cycle continued.

I let Emma know this was called polarized thinking. We see things one way: all or nothing, black or white with no grey. I asked Emma to think about how they could explore things differently. Rather than discussing what's wrong or right, she could get curious about her beliefs about timelines, getting things right, and responding to direction from a supervisor. When Emma came to a subsequent coaching session, here's what she had come up with:

- **Old way:** The focus is on the work. Your paperwork continues to be late, and that's a problem. What plan can we make to get your paperwork in on time?

- **New way:** The focus is on the person. I noticed (nonjudgmentally, instead of critically) that you missed the deadlines at the end of the month. Can we explore what's going on for you that prevents you from meeting those deadlines?

Emma realized she had had a strong value around meeting deadlines, often to the point of rigidity without consideration. The shift in perspective came when she realized that she'd been thinking the employees were missing deadlines because they were lazy and didn't care about her rules. Emma had been reading about assuming positive intent. She realized she could assume the employee wants to do their best. When we start with the assumption that they mean no harm, instead of convincing them they're doing things wrong, it changes the conversation's tone.

Here is another example of how my client Brenda pivoted from fear to confidence. Brenda told me that she hated board meetings because one of the board members had been nasty when she did Brenda's performance appraisal several years ago. Brenda still remembers feeling attacked by that board member. A meeting was coming up, and Brenda was dreading it.

Since that traumatizing meeting, Brenda distrusted that board member, leading to a tenuous relationship. Brenda struggles to work with this board member effectively.

I asked Brenda about that performance appraisal. Brenda indicated that the performance appraisal issue was something she wished she'd handled differently. Instead of reacting, getting defensive, and lashing out, she wishes she could have managed her emotions. She realized now that she had grown a lot since then. By using the Infinite Leadership Loop, by coming to coaching to pause and then ponder, Brenda realized her thoughts were full of an old storyline.

- Brenda had an old belief: "The board member doesn't think I'm competent."
- Brenda's perspective was that that board member didn't like her.
- Brenda's judgment was "I don't trust the board member."

Brenda also became more aware of her body sensations. Brenda would tense up whenever she had to engage with this board member. Brenda realized she felt incompetent and lacked confidence whenever she had to talk to that person. While pondering, Brenda looked at her thoughts, feelings, and body sensations as indicators of what was happening. Brenda increased her self-awareness.

Brenda became aware that she'd been holding onto old hurts, stories, and conflicts. She realized she had not allowed her relationship with her board member to grow and move past that incident ten years ago. She recognized this situation had been traumatic to her.

Once Brenda identified the old patterns of thoughts and feelings, we started looking at different perspectives, and Brenda could pivot. She chose to adopt a growth mindset, allowing her to dip into post-traumatic growth. Her new story looked like this:

- I have a lot more skills than I did back then.
- I am quite capable, competent, and effective at my job.
- I learned a lot from my past mistakes and often handle situations differently and more effectively now.

By the end of our coaching call, Brenda felt lighter and more confident. She was ready to proceed with a new mindset around this particular board member. Brenda and I prepared talking points so she could bravely discuss the current challenge, feeling more confident and certainly lighter without all that old baggage.

Now that you've paused and pondered, let's help you learn to proceed back into action with your people.

12

Proceed and People

ELF-REFLECTION AND creating an intention are only the beginning. After pausing and shifting your perspective, the next step is to proceed with courage and vulnerability and re-engage with your people. This may seem daunting, but it is necessary for growth and authentic leadership. We all know that an object at rest stays at rest. Therefore, if you want to move back into action, you have to get the ball rolling.

Step 4: Proceed

This step is often the hardest. As you access your inner wisdom, new insights, more conscious choices, and tune into your aspirational identity, you may be left with a new perspective, prompting you to take different actions or respond in an unusual way. That new behaviour may be contradictory to what you are used to. It may also be far from what those around you are accustomed to. That could be uncomfortable for you and them.

If we aren't careful, the discomfort can paralyze us. We freeze, not wanting to go to the next step. In a way, it feels better to stay right where we are, in that comfort zone that really isn't very comfortable. This is how we stay stuck in survival mode, settling for far too long.

Proceeding forward may mean you need to dial up your humility and say you are sorry or were wrong. It could mean you need to be more disciplined with yourself and others, setting better boundaries. You may have realized it's time to gather the courage to apply for a new job, cut the program, or make that call.

What will help you embrace courage and vulnerability as you proceed forward? Acknowledge your feelings, and name them to tame them. It's common to feel vulnerable when considering personal growth and change. Embrace these feelings as a natural part of the process and reframe vulnerability as a strength and a powerful act of courage. This step is all about working to adopt the mindset that vulnerability is a sign of strength, not weakness.

As women leaders, we are often our own harshest critics. When you feel the need to proceed with courage and vulnerability, practise self-compassion and recognize that you are human and that it's okay to feel uncertain at times. This is why it's so important to have your Character Development Plan. By keeping in mind who you are and who you are becoming, you'll have a guide and motivation to proceed.

Proceeding will often activate your moral courage. As I said earlier, moral courage is one of the fundamental traits of character driven leaders. If you want to lead your nonprofit with integrity, you must get used to using your moral compass. Let your moral compass guide your words, actions, and decisions. It will help you determine what is right and wrong for you as a leader (and as a person).

When you cancel your regularly scheduled supervision with someone, do you tell them it's because you have another more important meeting, you are exhausted, or because you can't stomach the conversation you have to have with them?

Which one is closest to the truth? This is a moral decision. It is about calling in courage.

To proceed, consider the essence of who you are. Go back to your VIA Character Strengths profile. Do you have any of the courage strengths in your top five or top ten? How can they help you move forward? Here is a quick overview of the character strengths associated with courage:

- **Bravery:** "I act on my convictions, and I face threats, challenges, difficulties, and pains despite my doubts and fears."

- **Honesty:** "I am honest to myself and to others; I try to present myself and my reactions accurately to each person; and I take responsibility for my actions."

- **Perseverance:** "I persist toward my goals despite obstacles, discouragements, or disappointments."

- **Zest:** "I feel vital and full of energy. I approach life feeling activated and enthusiastic."

Proceeding forward sometimes means taking no action at all, or non-action. Instead of reacting impulsively, such as storming into someone's office, sending out an abrupt email to the team, or hastily applying for a new position, you consciously choose to refrain from action. This might involve delaying a decision, abstaining from engaging in a conversation, or resisting the urge to send a message. By giving yourself space or redirecting your focus, you allow room for reflection and alternative perspectives, leading to a more thoughtful and strategic approach to developing your character. Non-action can be a powerful tool in your personal growth journey and character development.

Consider a micro-moment during a meeting when you feel provoked. Your immediate impulse might be to retaliate or assert yourself. However, by tuning in and reflecting in that moment, you may realize that simply nodding your head and actively listening could be the most effective course of action. Similarly, staying silent instead of immediately jumping in to give instructions or advice is another example of practising non-action.

Step 5: People

You can't say you have a strong reputation and lead with character in isolation. People are at the heart of nonprofit work. You can't build character without relationships. Every interaction, every collaboration, and every connection shapes the culture of your organization. It's through listening, understanding, and valuing the contributions of others that true leadership emerges. In nonprofit work, our impact is magnified by the strength of our team and the trust we build within it. You can have great intentions, but that doesn't mean you act on them.

- I meant to talk to Becky today.

- I was going to say thank you to John.

- I fully intended to get that report to you on time.

- I didn't mean to sound snarky.

- Ugh, it slipped my mind. I planned to do it.

- I wanted to go to that.

- I promise I'll get it to you before the end of the day.

- I hope to be there.

- I'll put it at the top of my priority list.

Without action, here is what you are really saying:

- I meant to talk to Becky today (but I didn't prioritize her over other tasks).

- I was going to say thank you to John (but I never got around to it).

- I fully intended to get that report to you on time (but I allowed an interruption to get in the way).

- I didn't mean to sound snarky (but I've had a bad day).

- Ugh, it slipped my mind. I planned to do it. (Can I make it up to you?)

- I wanted to go to that (but other things kept popping up, which mattered more.)

- I promise I'll get it to you before the end of the day (but I didn't because I make unrealistic promises).

- I hope to be there (but I'll probably miss it).

- I'll put it at the top of my priority list (until something else becomes a bigger priority).

How others describe you and your character is based on your actions, words, and behaviours. It is how others define you versus how you define yourself. You cultivate and grow others' perceptions of you with or without intention. The greater the intention, the higher the impact and satisfaction. Priorities matter. How you prioritize interactions with people and the tasks you perform influences others' perceptions of your character.

Think about what others would say about how you engage with them when you give feedback or address concerns. How about when you complete staff performance reviews? How often do you share recognition and appreciation? These are all examples of how you conduct yourself. Actions speak louder than words. One-on-one meetings that look like the following will result in a reputation you probably don't want:

- Meeting inconsistently with team members

- Losing track of agenda items and issues of concern and not following up on key items

- Lacking the structure to raise areas of concern without making a big deal about them, so you often postpone those conversations

- Struggling with accountability and follow-up between meetings for you and your team members

Seeing these patterns show up for you gives you a place to return to the Infinite Leadership Loop and create a new experience for you and your people. Perhaps you may see the indications of poor team morale. Their attitude sucks, and maybe yours as well! "Whatever! If no one else cares, why should I?" You can tell that overall mood affects people's mental and physical health. People call in sick when you know they just don't want to be there. Your turnover rates aren't looking good. You lost two staff members last month. The good ones are quitting, moving on, or getting out fast. And you are suffering!

It's affecting you big time, too, as you sink deeper and deeper into survival mode. You dread going to work. When you are at the office, you avoid people as much as possible, keeping yourself busy in meetings, behind closed doors, or travelling. But out of sight isn't out of mind. It hasn't gone away, and you know it. Even though you've been trying to pretend it's not a problem, you still know it's there.

- You see the cliques during meetings but don't address them.

- You notice the tension between team members but hope it will disappear.

- You watch with frustration as the office gossip continues. It feels like you're back in junior high, but you worry that it will blow up in your face if you attempt to deal with it.

But you know, don't you, that it will only worsen if you don't deal with it. So, you pause, ponder, and pivot. But at some point, you need to actually proceed if you want to prevent your whole group of people from becoming toxic.

Before reading this book, you may not have had the confidence to address your team's morale. You may not have thought you could handle the inner work and emotional control to re-engage with your team and earn their respect. But you do!

I know that feeling all too well. Remember, I had a mess of a team, too, and I didn't know how to handle it. The problem was the more I avoided it, waited for someone else to fix it, or blamed my staff's immaturity, the worse it got. It took time for me to develop my character. At one point, the toxicity was so bad I went on stress leave.

Moral courage is one of the fundamental traits of character driven leaders. If you want to lead your nonprofit with integrity, you must get used to using your moral compass.

Another time, a team member went on leave and then quit because I'm pretty sure she didn't want to face the ugly mess our team had become. Both times, I had to step up confidently, take the reins, and boost our team morale.

Here's the thing: nothing will change in your team until you start to make changes. Waiting, wishing, or hoping won't change it, nor will blaming, finger-pointing, or criticizing others. Team morale changes when you take the lead on changing it.

As you move forward with courage and vulnerability, take a moment to ground yourself mentally. Remind yourself of your values, strengths, and the purpose behind the conversation. This mental preparation will help you approach the interaction with clarity and confidence. Whether empathy is on your list of traits to cultivate or not, practising empathy fosters understanding and builds trust, even in challenging conversations. In your mind, pause and consider how the other person might perceive the situation. You may even validate their feelings.

Vulnerable Narration

One of the most challenging tasks we face as leaders is navigating difficult conversations. These moments can be tense and uncomfortable; however, within this discomfort lies an opportunity for connection and growth. At these times, you can practise vulnerable narration.

Vulnerable narration is openly acknowledging the difficulty of a conversation and talking our way through it as if we are both in the conversation and narrating it simultaneously. It allows us to bravely express our emotions and uncertainties, creating a space of authenticity and trust where meaningful dialogue can thrive.

Vulnerability is often misunderstood as a sign of weakness, but in reality, it is one of our greatest strengths. When we allow ourselves to be vulnerable, we open the door to deeper connections, authentic relationships, and meaningful dialogue. Vulnerability is the foundation of trust, and it is through vulnerability that we can truly connect with others on a human level.

To begin the conversation with this level of vulnerability, start with a statement acknowledging the difficulty of the topic for you and perhaps for them. For example, "I want to discuss something that's been on my mind, and I have to admit, it's not easy for me to bring it up."

Continue to have the conversation while inserting narrative statements as you go. Remember to focus on expressing your own thoughts and feelings using "I" statements. This helps you take ownership of your emotions and avoid placing blame on the other person. For instance, say "I feel anxious about discussing this because I'm concerned about how it might impact our relationship."

Mastering the art of vulnerable narration requires courage, honesty, and self-awareness. This kind of conversation will require your moral courage and test your emotional intelligence as you work to maintain composure, even if you're feeling nervous or emotional. But your confidence to move forward, even with vulnerability, will help to reassure the other person and keep the dialogue constructive.

While it's important to acknowledge any mistakes or shortcomings, avoid over-apologizing during the conversation. Instead, focus on expressing your intentions and commitment to resolving the issue.

Narration involves openly acknowledging the challenges and discomforts present in the dialogue. It is about expressing our thoughts, feelings, and uncertainties in a genuine and transparent manner. Narration serves as a bridge between individuals, creating a safe space for open communication and mutual understanding.

By narrating our vulnerability, we pave the way for deeper connections, greater empathy, and, ultimately, positive transformation. It creates the engagement in our team we need to build a magnetic workplace.

When I was explaining vulnerable narration to a group, one of the participants, Shannon, used the following example to emphasize the power of vulnerable narration for her. Shannon and a co-worker were driving back from training at night during a snowstorm. Winter driving is not Shannon's comfort zone, and she felt nervous. As

Shannon drove, she narrated out loud what she was doing: "I'm just taking my foot off the gas as it feels slightly slippery here. I can still see the centre line, so I'm keeping my eye on it." It was done unconsciously, but in hindsight, it let her peer know that while she felt uncomfortable, Shannon knew what she was doing and was using her skills in a tense situation. Shannon said not only did this appear to help her peer feel more confident in Shannon's driving, but it also gave her peer permission to narrate what she was doing as well: "I can see the white line on the edge of the road, and I'll keep my eye on it while I watch for wildlife."

You can see how narrating gave Shannon and her peer a tool to be vulnerable while navigating a tense time. It built trust, created openness, and helped them both feel they could share their journey of the tenuous trip.

My client Natalie told me she used vulnerable narrating to explain her silence in team meetings. She said to her team: "I'm going to be quiet while I wait for input. I am uncomfortable with silence, and you all know I usually jump in before you've had time to think things through and share your ideas. So I'm over here zipping my lips for a minute, even though it feels awkward!"

Here are some introductory statements you can use to get you started in a difficult conversation:

- I've been reflecting on something lately, and I want to share it with you, even though it's not easy for me to talk about.

- There's something important I've been holding back, and I think it's time for us to address it, even though it's uncomfortable for me.

- I've been wrestling with how to bring this up, but I believe it's necessary for us to have an open discussion about it.

- I've been feeling a bit uneasy about this topic, but I believe honesty is crucial for our relationship, so I want to talk about it.

- I've been avoiding this conversation because it's challenging for me, but I realize it's important for us to address it head-on.

- I've been struggling with how to approach this, but I value our relationship too much to keep avoiding it.

- I've been feeling apprehensive about discussing this, but I believe it's necessary for our growth as individuals and as a team.

Leading with character and authenticity is not always easy, but it's essential for building trust, inspiring others, and creating meaningful change. By taking the time to pause, reflect, and then engage with courage and vulnerability, you can navigate even the toughest conversations with grace and wisdom if you choose to. Let's talk about your choice points now.

13

Use Your Choice Points

CHOICE POINTS are pivotal moments along your journey where you can pause and make decisions. These decisions are normally made unconsciously, as reactions rather than thoughtful responses. Our aim is to bring more consciousness to these moments, because decisions are crucial for character building. They define who you are in relation to others in the world. Too often, we miss moments when we make those decisions, letting them be unconscious instead of conscious. The moments of decision are our choice points.

A choice point is an opportunity for you to choose

- what you are saying or not saying
- what you are doing or not doing
- who you are being in the process

Character is developed in micro-moments via your micro-decisions. Most often, we are unaware of our decisions and, as a result, make unconscious decisions that don't align with who we want to be or the impact we want to have. We need to become more aware of those choice points, so when we make our decisions, they are more intentional and thought out. When you use your choice points intentionally, you'll make better decisions that help you develop your character, and you'll be leading with authenticity and integrity.

If you are stuck in survival mode, you may feel like your choices are limited and you may be attributing what you are experiencing to external factors. But the truth is we all have choices, even if they come with consequences. Feeling like a victim of circumstance robs you of self-control, as external forces dictate your life.

I was in martyr mode during my two big leadership lows. Maybe you know this mode. I believed it was everyone else's fault and I felt powerless. Martyrs wait for change while refusing to take action themselves, often seeking sympathy rather than solutions. By relinquishing power to external circumstances, they perpetuate frustration and suffering, hindering personal growth and leadership development. I got out of my leadership lows when I started to take my power back and use my choice points more wisely.

Regardless of everything else around you, you have the ability to change your thoughts. Your thoughts, your beliefs, and your perspective are how you interpret things. They give meaning to events, and you can choose to change your interpretations, even in the midst of chaos, overwhelm, and spiralling emotions.

Character development requires controlling your thoughts and behaviours and taking responsibility for developing yourself. That isn't always easy. We've become so accustomed to habitual patterns of thought that we point fingers, blame, and shove responsibility for how we are feeling away. What's more, we've found value in thinking this way—we get sympathy for it!

Reacting as a victim of the situation can often lead to complaining, venting, and gossiping about it to those around you, as your team culture dips dangerously close to toxic. Sadly, it also leaves you with immense internal frustration, turmoil, and suffering. Either way you look at it, it sucks! And what's more, it does not develop the characteristics in you that will make you a leader with a strong character.

Character driven leaders understand that waiting for change is futile; true transformation begins with a shift in mindset and perspective. You do that by making good decisions, and you do that by being aware of your choice points.

Throughout your day, you encounter numerous choice points that shape how your day goes, how your relationships develop, how your work impacts the world, and how you feel. These choice points are opportunities to make decisions that often go unnoticed in the hustle and bustle of daily responsibilities. By neglecting to recognize these decision points, we as leaders miss opportunities to choose to cultivate our character and steer our organizations and teams in the right direction.

Often, we think we are making decisions when we really aren't. Instead, we make excuses about why we're doing what we're doing. We point fingers ("The funder needs it"), resign to martyr syndrome ("I'm the only one who can do it"), or get caught up in survival mode, just running around the hamster wheel.

Too often we make decisions by default. Rather than making a decision, we put our attention, focus, and resources into reacting to

- the biggest fire
- the loudest person
- the crisis of the day
- the most important person
- the issue most likely to blow up
- the drama that is triggering us the most

These Whac-A-Mole decisions are made with tunnel vision. Stress causes us to narrow our focus and often make fear-based decisions. Tight and tense is not the best way to make decisions.

When we aren't making choices, we tend to follow this path: "If *A* happens, I do *B*." That's not a decision. It's a habit. Just because you get invited to a meeting doesn't mean you need to attend it. Just because someone asks for "just a minute" doesn't mean you must say yes. Just because it came into your inbox doesn't mean you are the one to deal with it or you need to deal with it today.

We say we are making a choice, but really we often aren't deciding anything. So, when we say "The choice is either I do the work or the work doesn't get done," that's not a choice. That is a victim mentality. Or if we say "Either I stay late or do it in the morning," what are you deciding? Which punishment to take? It's an either/or, with neither option being optimal. They're two sides of the same coin.

Using choice points allows us to move from reactive behaviour—firefighting and crisis management—to proactive, intentional decision-making about our actions and communication. Instead of acting as a high-alert Whac-A-Mole leader, you pause and relax. Then ponder with a curious perspective. Be open to new ways of seeing things, and then use those new perspectives to proceed with conversations with your people with moral courage.

Decisions Drive Character

Our decisions shape us and shape others' views of us. Do your decisions match what you want that view to be? For your decisions to intentionally drive character development, they must be made deliberately. Ask yourself if you are intentionally choosing something. We need to turn unconscious decisions into a pause that results in a conscious choice.

Most of our choice points go by unnoticed. It is by pausing, slowing down, and recognizing your choice points that you gain the opportunity to decide how you will engage, live, and lead with a strong character. More often, you'll be contemplating before doing something: "Is this choice a reflection of who I am and who I am becoming?" Doing this allows you to live and lead with intention. Remember, pause counts twice!

While decisions build character, we must also recognize that some decisions are hard to make, which is why we avoid them. The word "decide" originally meant to "cut off." When we decide one thing, we are cutting off something else, another option, person, or event. That's why it's important to remember that self-reflection builds character. Be sure you are cutting off the right thing. Using your choice points wisely to make a decision helps you align with what's important, even when it's hard.

Choice Points Around the Loop

Your choice points are everywhere around you and at each turn in the Infinite Leadership Loop. When you intentionally make a decision, you must first pause, slow down, and then ponder. By contemplating the paths ahead of you, you pivot, realizing you have more than an either/or approach. You see options, opportunities, and outcomes you can create. Finally, after purposefully deciding, you proceed back into action with your people.

Taking time for self-reflection and introspection via the Infinite Leadership Loop allows leaders to identify decision points that might have otherwise slipped through the cracks. You can seize these pivotal moments around the Infinite Leadership Loop and harness them for character development by heightening your awareness. Imagine that you need to address a problem with a difficult team member. This framework gives you a multitude of choice points so that you handle it in a way that aligns with who you want to become.

Pause: Will I choose to pause or not?

Ponder: Will I choose to engage in intentional self-reflection and envision the outcome I desire? These questions will help you choose the ideal path:

- What am I choosing to envision?
- Am I choosing to build or dissipate energy?
- What emotions am I choosing to cultivate?
- Am I choosing to hang on to emotions or allow myself to move through them and create a new experience?

These small unconscious
decisions often paint
a picture of the type of
leader you are. **Choose the
image you're painting.**

Pivot: Am I choosing to pivot my perspective about this person, project, or problem?

Proceed: What behaviour or non-action am I choosing as I move into my outer world?

People: How am I choosing to engage with the people around me?

Each choice point along the Infinite Leadership Loop allows you to move closer to or further away from your aspirational identity. The strategy is to use your choice points to make better decisions based on your Character Development Plan. Aligned decisions happen when you plan first. You will become more conscious of your choice points and thus make decisions more effectively with increased alignment with your values, growing both more in tune with who you really are and more in tune with your goals.

Conscious choices and decisions are instrumental to your success. It's not just the big decisions. It is also the micro-decisions. What may seem inconsequential sets a series of events in motion. Those events lead to more choices, all of which change how you manage yourself, your role, your people, and your impact.

Here's an example. Someone lied to me the other day. It was a lie to cover up a lie. I knew it right away. I'm not sure that they knew it though. Maybe not consciously. I think it's a habit for them. Regardless of whether they knew they'd lied to me, their habit of lying caused me to lose another measure of trust in them. Trust, one of the foundations of leadership, is built by leaders' decisions, one decision at a time. Each decision builds on the previous decision, solidifying how much someone feels you are trustworthy. However, one seemingly small decision can bring trust crashing down.

These small unconscious decisions often paint a picture of the type of leader you are. Choose the image you're painting. That requires you to be more conscious of your decision-making, especially your micro-decisions. Micro-decisions are made all day and are rarely seen as decisions because they appear to be habits. But make no doubt about it, you can choose differently.

Consider these examples of micro-decisions:

- Picking your phone up several times during a conversation to check your notifications, email, or social media. Or choosing to leave your phone in the other room or in your pocket.

- Rolling your eyes when someone complains again about something that's been discussed multiple times. Or taking a deep breath before you respond to a triggering comment.

- Snapping a little more aggressively than you meant to at someone. Or grabbing some food to refuel yourself before you get hangry.

- Creating a list of things that need to be "addressed" before going into staff supervision. Or reminding yourself of your employee's strengths before a conversation with them and considering how you can use those strengths to develop their competence.

- Keeping your head down and praying no one will talk to you when you walk down the hall to your office. Or smiling and making eye contact with people, responding to bids for your attention with "I don't have time to chat about that now. Can we do it at two p.m.? I'll have fifteen minutes then."

- Choosing when to keep working on your project. Or getting up and touching base with your employees.

- Deciding to stay late today. Or going home on time.

Micro-decisions shape your character, paint a picture of who you are, and tell others about the type of leader you are. Each time you pause and use your choice points, you'll become increasingly conscious of the micro-decisions you are painting.

Take some time to consider if your micro-decisions paint the picture of the leader you want to be. If not, what do you need to do to become more conscious, and how will you choose differently?

Decision-Making Frameworks

To use your choice points wisely, you must give yourself time to think. Incorporate a practice in your daily routine by anticipating choice points in the morning or reflecting on them in the evening. We often miss our choice points because they are micro-moments and micro-decisions. We need to be more conscious of these micro-moments and use them as character development points. This way, you can ensure that your decisions align with your beliefs, values, goals, and vision.

To make your decisions with more certainty, develop decision-making criteria based on priorities, time constraints, existing resources, interests, skills, and expectations along with values, traits, and strengths. Such criteria provide a solid foundation for making better choices that align with your character and support your team.

A quick decision-making framework may look something like this:

1 What is the choice I am making?
2 What criteria am I using to make that choice?
3 What are the consequences of this choice?

Another framework is to ask yourself, "If I decide to do this, what am I saying yes to, and what am I saying no to?" When you say you will stay late to catch up on emails, you may be saying yes to emails, but no to supper with the family or no to having time to do your workout. How does that impact you and those close to you? By saying yes to answering a team member's questions, you may be saying no to creating a boundary for your uninterrupted focus time.

A character driven framework requires you to ask yourself questions to ensure that your decisions are based on your character strengths and aspirational identity. An overarching character question to ask when you are making a decision is "Is this decision a statement of who I am and who I am becoming?" This question allows you to reconnect with your values, the type of leader you aspire to be, and the impact you choose to have. You have choice points. Be sure you use them with intention.

Now that you've embraced who you are, pondered your potential via your aspirational identity, created a plan, and learned how to engage in endless growth, let's make sure it sticks. Coming up are six practices to help you become a character driven leader.

PART FOUR

MAKING IT
STICK

14

Lead with Learning

TO HELP YOU lead with character, there are six practices to incorporate into your life and leadership. These practices will help you build, adapt, and rebuild your Character Development Plan as you grow. Learn to use them and practise them for the rest of your life.

The first practice is to always be leading yourself with a learner's mind. The number one fear women leaders have is not being competent, not measuring up, looking like an idiot, stumbling over your words, failing, or making a big mistake. Women are afraid of looking like they are incompetent. Competence comes from knowledge and skill development, which helps to overcome imposter syndrome. So, you need to always be learning. However, I'd venture to guess that you have never been trained in several areas you are currently struggling with.

When you advance into a leadership position, you suddenly must understand more than the mechanics of the job. You are no longer only concerned with the duties of a frontline role. You must discover how to get people to work together, motivate them, and navigate the ongoing drama between co-workers. Now that everyone's eyes are always on you, you need to figure out how to be calm and composed even when you feel like freaking out, falling apart, or running away. You are perhaps thrust into more networking events and contract negotiation meetings. And you're now responsible for running meetings that not only get the agenda topics covered but also engage the team.

If you did have some training in those areas, consider the hands-on learning you've had to apply that knowledge, if any. Did you have a teacher, guide, or mentor giving you feedback as you applied that knowledge? In most organizations, you are sent on training and expected to return skilled. Yet there is often a wide chasm between learning the theory of a skill and being efficient at using that skill. Rarely will you be given direction, support, or help to get there.

While you may worry that you aren't competent, there are likely many areas where you are very competent. The problem is the lack of courage to apply your skills, knowledge, or talents. Many of us also wait for confidence to show up before we step out. But the truth is, all these aspects work together. Let me explain.

Competence is having the skills or ability. Courage is being willing to use those skills even if you are not very proficient or feel afraid. Confidence comes *after* you've had some experience using the new skill. This is the competence-confidence spiral. Your confidence rises as your competence increases, and you have the courage to practise. Each time you learn, practise, and apply your skill, your confidence builds, helping you overcome imposter syndrome.

As you grow your leadership and develop your character, you must also develop skills to fill your learning gaps. You must identify these (with self-awareness) and put them into your Character Development Plan (as goals). Consider these examples of learning gaps and suggestions for development:

- Reading about great communication skills is different from using them in the heat of the moment when tensions are high, and you're swamped. Mindfulness practice may help you in these situations.

- You may get results, but are they the right results? And at what cost? If this is an issue for you, learning about strategic thinking and planning may benefit you.

- Building a cohesive team is fine until you have one of "those" employees. Discovering how to manage your emotions and maintain your composure may be an important component to add to your Character Development Plan.

- You might be one of the many leaders who struggle to get things done and know it's because you need to set better boundaries with staff. If it weren't for the interruptions, you'd have more time to focus on important but neglected stuff. Cal Newport's book *Deep Work* could be your learning strategy.

Remember when we talked about the fundamentals of leadership? Learning is one of them. Learning doesn't end with formal education; it's a lifelong pursuit. To grow professionally, we must be willing to grow personally. To become a strong leader with strength of character, you must be willing to grow yourself from the inside out.

Lifelong Learning

Mental performance coach Brian Cain says, "When you stop getting better, you start getting bitter." When I look back on my journey, I realize my lack of learning was part of what got me into trouble. When my programs grew so fast, I put learning on the back burner. And when I stopped learning, I got bitter.

I'd always been a learner. As I've mentioned, on my Clifton-Strengths Assessment, my top talent is learner. When I was new to leadership, I took courses on supervising staff. I listened to CDs while travelling for work to learn about leadership, time management, and team dynamics. I worked on my leadership degree course by course, taking eight years to complete it. When I wanted to support my clients, I dove deep into the world of fetal alcohol spectrum disorder, to the point of becoming part of the diagnostic and assessment team. That's when we got the big contract. That's when I got too busy to learn. And that's when I started on my path to bitterness, resentment, and falling out of character. Somewhere along the way, I stopped journaling, became too busy to read, and even stopped training as work got really busy.

Not everyone loves learning for learning's sake. If this is you, you may need to tap into something inside you that helps you turn on your learning muscles. Learning is foundational, and you shouldn't feel forced to do it; you should feel drawn to it. It may be curiosity about how to live more aligned with your values, the desire to be a better leader, or the urge to understand how to motivate others that help activate this practice.

Beyond skill development, learning about yourself can help you align with your future self-identity. But first, you need to unpack everything to make sense of it. This is not about therapy or reliving your childhood, although you may include some of that in your Character Development Plan. Many of us can benefit greatly from therapy. Learning about what shaped us also helps to make sense of our current belief system. Because this belief system is largely unconscious, it is only by unpacking our layers of beliefs that we can begin to understand them and choose which ones we want to keep as we cultivate the character traits we desire.

Learning can take the form of mentorship or coaching; look around you for leaders, peers, and people in the sector you may want to learn from. I learned a lot from a government funder, who often took me under his wing and gave me advice. He'd call me up and say, "You may want to…" Initially, I didn't understand why he did that. Later, I realized he saw potential in me. I learned to call and ask him for advice, suggestions, and feedback.

You may also need to get comfortable asking others to help you learn and grow. When you ask for help to learn, people experience that differently than when you ask for them to do it for you. Be clear that you are learning and growing and looking for help doing that.

One of the best ways to learn from others is from afar. Your mentor can be someone whose books you read or podcasts you listen to.

Competence is having the skills or ability. Courage is being willing to use those skills even if you are not very proficient or feel afraid. **Confidence comes *after* you've had some experience using the new skill.**

Your mentor doesn't have to be alive. I learned a lot about character from reading about Eleanor Roosevelt and from many of the books penned by C.S. Lewis. I'm often learning from historical figures like Epictetus, Seneca, and Marcus Aurelius, who were all Stoics who believed they don't control the world around them, only how they respond. A good reminder for leaders.

When you learn about leadership from traditional leadership books, please run what you read through the lens of your aspirational identity. Do the concepts align with who you are and who you are becoming? You get to pick and choose which parts of your reading to assimilate.

As Lisa Feldman Barrett suggests, our emotions are predictions based on memories, and sometimes our leadership experiences are limited. Expanding your reading and learning helps create new predictions in the brain.

Beyond traditional leadership books, I've delved into other genres. I dove deep into *The Purpose Driven Life* by Rick Warren, which again gave me so much insight into developing character. Mindfulness training and learning about willpower increased my emotional intelligence, and learning about improv has helped me in conflict situations.

As Barrett writes in *Seven and a Half Lessons About the Brain*, "It's impossible to change your past, but right now, with some effort, you can change how your brain will predict the future. You can invest a little time and energy to learn new ideas. You can curate new experiences. You can try new activities. Everything you learn today seeds your brain to predict differently tomorrow."

How to Fit in Learning

Yes, you have a busy schedule. And you must take back your power of choice here. Learning needs to be done on purpose, guided by your learning goals. It's about becoming aware of your choice points and then using them to fit learning in with these mindset shifts.

First, you need to shift from thinking that this type of learning and growth is extra work that should be done outside of work time to thinking that this learning *is* the work of leadership. With that mindset, you'll pivot how you manage your training and begin to own your learning. You will drive what, when, and how you learn by using your choice points with intention.

Next, you must shift from believing you need more time to learn to believing that some learning can be done in micro-moments. While you may be able to carve out longer times for learning, many busy leaders don't have that luxury. Much of your learning must be done in small windows of time.

Finally, you must choose to make learning a priority. If you have time to scroll, you have time to learn. If you choose to prioritize cleaning the house, you'll put learning on the back burner. If you keep putting focusing on fires over focusing on learning, you'll stay in survival mode. The choice is yours.

15

Mould Your Mindset

THE SECOND PRACTICE to help you develop your character is all about moulding your mindset. Our mindset is our current way of thinking. Consider the saying "frame of mind": the frame is the lens through which we look. Mindsets are patterns of thought seen through that frame, which lead to perspectives, and we may need to pivot from these perspectives. Our mindset is our attitude toward life, events, others, and ourselves. Your mindset might be stuck in one of these recurring thought patterns:

- This is way too hard.
- It has to be perfect!
- I never have enough time.
- Of course, no one ever wants to help.

How you view things determines how you do things. What you think about yourself shapes your identity and impacts your conduct. But your mindset is more than one thought: it's a pattern of thoughts and your propensity to think about things in that way. Thus, you must be extra careful about how your view determines your identity and your conduct. If you don't adjust your mindset appropriately, your thoughts and views will prevent you from shaping your character as you desire.

We all experience different feelings, emotions, and moods called "states." These are temporary emotional conditions in response to specific situations. They can include feelings of happiness, stress, excitement, or frustration, which can fluctuate throughout the day.

As we've discussed, learning to manage your moods effectively is an important part of emotional intelligence, and moods or affect, as Barrett explains, are one part of how emotions are constructed. If you are cranky in the morning and that mood lingers all day, you'll likely feel impatient when someone hands you a poorly written report.

Mindsets are the thinking pieces. The thoughts, beliefs, and attitudes we hold about ourselves, our abilities, and the world around us shape how we perceive and interpret events and how we approach challenges and opportunities. These beliefs and attitudes create our mindsets, determining our approach to ourselves, others, and the world around us.

While I may feel creative at times, that doesn't mean I am naturally creative. A creative mindset means looking at challenges through the lens of creativity. How can we creatively sort through this? Just because I may be naturally creative doesn't mean I always have a mindset of creativity. On long days, when I'm edging close to burning out, I may forget to flex my creativity muscles. But if I want to be known for being a leader who thinks through problems creatively, I need to do the work to set my mindset on thinking creatively.

In the ponder step, I encouraged you to consider states, traits, and mindsets: What are your thoughts and feelings? Who is the you that is feeling and thinking these things?

- I'm angry after thinking they lied to me.

- I'm naturally honest and expect it in others.

- It triggers me when they only share half the story, and I think they purposefully keep details from me.

The catch is that some days, you may choose to be more open and curious about why they only shared some details, and you'll ask questions. On other days, you may react defensively and confrontationally, potentially escalating the situation. Doing the work to mould your mindset so you are curious when facing what you perceive as dishonesty will move you closer to having the reputation you desire.

Your Mindset as a Setpoint

To help you think of your mindset as a setpoint, consider things we set at a specific point because we want them to stay there: our thermostat, the radio dial, the position of our car seats, or the oven temperature when we bake. I know from leadership experience about setpoints in the office. I had one staff member who was going through menopause and struggling with the temperature that everyone else wanted the thermostat set at. When she broke into the locked box I had installed on the thermostat and turned the air conditioning on in winter, it caused major frustration for the team and me.

I was the one who had to have yet another difficult conversation about something we'd already discussed. At that point, I hadn't experienced menopause, so my perspective was different than it would be now. Let me tell you, I did not exercise patience and compassion as that younger version of myself! And that affected my reputation.

Our mindset can be seen as a setpoint—the current state of our mind. Often we are stuck there, and even when we move away from that setpoint, we naturally revert to it. Talking to a peer, you might bemoan your workload, and she reminds you that you can handle it. You agree: "Yeah, I've got this." But before you hang up the call with her, your mind returns to the same point you were at before the call, and you get stuck there.

- How will I manage?
- I'll never get this done.
- This isn't going to work.
- There is no way I'll finish it.

Round and round, we go on the same track, stuck in a rut. The neural pathways in your brain become deep grooves through repetition. Rumination teaches your body what to predict, says Barrett. We become entrenched in one way of thinking. Getting out of our mindsets takes effort; that's the work of moulding a new mindset. It's shaping and reshaping your thoughts until they become your new pattern of thoughts, a new setpoint.

Write your thoughts down or say them out loud. When you hear or read them, you can analyze them and rewrite them. I often cross words out in thoughts I've written down and change them to reflect the mindset I am cultivating. At times, I'll rewrite a thought with a completely different focus, perhaps from a victim mentality to taking responsibility for my situation or from looking back to looking forward.

By rewriting thoughts, you are rerouting them. Think of a vine that can grow and trail willy-nilly; a gardener will tie the vine so that it grows in the direction they'd like. Tying vines is like managing your thoughts. When you learn to contain them in the mindset you want, you get the outcome you want.

Moulding your mindset requires you to shift your whole pattern of thinking and helps you adjust your mindset's dial. Think of a challenge you are currently experiencing and ask yourself:

- What is my dial tuned to?
- Where am I setting my mind?
- What temperature am I set at?
- What might be a better setpoint for this challenge?

To mould your mindset, first evaluate your current operating system. Your internal operating system is what makes you, you. In *Scaling Leadership*, the authors describe your internal operating system as

- your mental models
- your decision-making system

- your meaning-making system
- your inner beliefs and assumptions
- your level of awareness and emotional intelligence

These are all things I encourage you to consider when crafting your Character Development Plan. Most leaders continue to expand their responsibilities, roles, and expectations, but they never upgrade their internal operating system. Start by looking at your aspirational identity and create the framework for the kind of operating system your future self has.

Let me share an example of working to upgrade our internal operating system. On a coaching call with Phoebe, she wanted help with a staff member she was having challenges with. She mentioned a difficult conversation she'd had over Zoom. I asked her if her camera had been on as her goal was to be more courageous and honest with her employees by turning on her camera more frequently. Phoebe smirked and shook her head no.

I reminded Phoebe of our previous discussion that having cameras off or on is not a switch. It's a dial. So perhaps she doesn't start a meeting with her camera on. But by really tuning into her internal operating system, she'll lead with her values and strengths. When she senses something is off, a bit more sensitive, or there is a need to connect deeply, her internal operating system will guide her and give her the courage to say, "Hey, can we turn the cameras on for a few minutes?" That's an upgrade to her operating system.

Next, assess where you are. Look at your inner world and see which parts work well and which need to be updated. Take time to examine your values, beliefs, decision-making system, and meaning-making system.

Let me share some notes I have written down on a cue card that I copied from a book years ago. (I wish I could remember the book and the author, but I can't. I suspect the author was Joan Borysenko.) I share it here, without proper attribution, because I think this is so important in helping us create our new operating system. The title on my cue card is "Inner Work."

How you view things **determines how you do things.**

- Our meaning-making system: What we use to make sense of the world.

- Our decision-making system: How we analyze, decide, and act.

- Our values, spiritual beliefs, level of self-awareness, and emotional intelligence—our mental models: We use these to understand reality, think, act, and create.

- Our initial beliefs and assumptions make up our personal identity—the system we use to know who we are and to define and deploy ourselves into circumstances.

To me, that sums up inner work. Awareness of character does not change character. You need to do inner work to understand your meaning-making system, know how you make decisions, and make sense of your mental modes. Going back and journaling about these points will help you.

If your current mindset is getting you into trouble or if someone regularly triggers you, it is time to mould your mindset.

- What new ways of thinking, being, and interacting will help you feel more confident, competitive, and in control?

- Where will you learn how to lead with these new mindsets and with this new confidence level to have the impact you desire?

Negativity Bias and Fixed Mindsets

If you want to practise moving the needle, these two mindsets are ones to watch out for. Many of us get stuck in negativity bias and in a fixed mindset.

Our brains are wired to notice and remember negative experiences more easily; our negativity bias has us looking for what is wrong and keeping our focus there. The problem is we spend too much time looking for problems instead of our or others' potential.

When you catch yourself thinking pessimistically, challenge your negative thoughts by rewriting them. Ask yourself if there's another way to look at the situation or if you're being too hard on yourself. Then rewrite these negative thoughts.

Try seeing the good in challenges. This is where we activate our post-traumatic growth. Start a gratitude, positivity, or good news journal, and beyond journaling about life in general, try seeing the good in different work situations. Keep creating a new path for your thoughts. This takes effort because your mind wants to keep returning to the rut of negative thoughts.

Write down, for example, that a staff member helped clean up the board room after a particularly long team training session. Note that you are grateful that you had to make a really tough decision today because it allowed you to practise your new decision-making framework.

Work to move the needle gradually. Thinking positive thoughts is more challenging than it sounds. Rather than conceptualizing it as flipping a switch, think of it as a dial. You'll want to turn it step by step. Too often, we try to shift from "I hate this staff member" to "I love them" or "My job sucks" to "It's the best job in the world." Try to move through shades of feelings, emotions, and thoughts. Rather than just telling yourself it will be fine, try:

- I'm scared to address this issue.

- I'm willing to let go of the fear and learn how to handle it.

- I'm curious to learn strategies for handling situations like this.

Can you feel less rigidity in your body and more openness when you gradually shift emotions? Remember, moulding your mindset takes time, so your thoughts will continue to evolve.

- I'm learning that my emotions play a big role in how I see situations.

- I'm excited to train in emotional intelligence.

- I'm still afraid of messing it up.

- I'm learning to feel better about mistakes, failures, and growth.

- I'm willing to practise the skills I'm learning.

- This situation still sucks, but I'm appreciating how it's growing my confidence.

We can also get stuck in a fixed mindset. If you stay stuck in a fixed mindset, you'll stagnate, and so will your team and organization. A fixed mindset is the belief that your qualities and your team's are carved in stone. Who you are is who you are, period.

Adopting a growth mindset helps you to see your and your employees' basic qualities can be cultivated through effort. As we've learned, leadership is a growth journey that requires continuous self-development. With a growth mindset, you believe that we all can grow through effort, hard work, and time.

To adopt a growth mindset, you can be creative. When faced with a challenge, imagine opening your desk drawer and seeing a bunch of eyeglasses. Remember to choose your lens carefully. Rummage through them and grab the one that says opportunities.

Another strategy to develop a growth mindset is to create a mistake and failure list: add the mistakes and failures you or the team made to the list each week, and reflect on what you can learn from the experiences and how you can improve in the future. How did or could you grow due to that mistake or failure?

Failure: I lost it at the board meeting today. I started crying and couldn't get my point across.

Growth: I learned that I can't go from one meeting to the next all day and expect myself to hold it together in a meeting at the end of the day. I've scheduled hour-long breaks at 3 p.m. on the days we have board meetings at 4 p.m. so I can regroup, rest, and recharge.

You may also want to adopt the habit of saying "yet" at the end of sentences that feel as though they are sliding back into a fixed mindset. "Yet" becomes your growth mindset hack. We set our dial to say "yet" when we hear ourselves say "We just aren't there." "Yet" evokes the sense that we will, in fact, get there. It encourages us to see what it might be like when we do get there. For example, knowing you need more time to think, you might say to yourself, "I don't know how to create more space in my calendar for thinking ... yet."

Often when we are overthinking, we get caught in thought spirals. These spirals can carry us away for minutes, hours, and even days before we realize we've been hooked and dragged around. A student of mine said that she thinks her way back out when she gets stuck in overthinking and catches herself. She asks herself:

- What was the thought before that?
- Why did I think that?

By backtracking her thoughts, she can trace her way back to the original thought that sent her spiralling. This retracing process allows her to train her brain and reroute her thinking.

Moulding your mindset takes place in the ebb and flow of the Infinite Leadership Loop. Be intentional about how you create your mindset in your Character Development Plan.

16

Call In Curiosity

THE THIRD PRACTICE to help you become a character driven leader is to call in curiosity. As Bill Scott and I said in our work together, curiosity is the fuel that propels you through the five parts of the Infinite Leadership Loop—pause, ponder, pivot, proceed, and people—and it deepens your understanding of the relationship between your inner work and external interactions. Curiosity helps you develop your character by driving you to learn about your thoughts, beliefs, feelings, body sensations, mindsets, narratives, and subsequent reactions.

The first problem is that we often avoid being curious. Being inquisitive, interested, or investigative can also be called being meddling, prying, nosy, snoopy, or navel-gazing. Those seem like less than desirable character traits to cultivate. We've been socialized to think that sticking our noses in someone else's business is wrong, and we've been discouraged from exploring difficult things in our own inner world.

The second problem with curiosity is that we often mistakenly believe that a leader is supposed to know everything. Admitting we don't seems to demonstrate incompetence, which is often our biggest fear. Tied to imposter syndrome is the fear that someone will figure out we don't know something, call us out, and we will feel shame wash over us. I get it. And yet, if you want to grow yourself, you'll need to call in curiosity often. Being willing to be vulnerable and curious shows strength, humility, adaptability, courage, and perseverance. Are any of those on the list of traits you want to cultivate?

Curiosity isn't a fleeting interest; it's a mindset—a willingness to slow down, question assumptions, and explore possibilities. Here in lies the third problem: we believe we don't have time for that. Stuck in survival mode, we are focused on solving the problem at hand, putting out the fire that just flared up, dealing with the crisis of the day, and preventing damage. We are looking for a quick fix or the easiest solution. Slowing down isn't part of that agenda.

In the pondering stage, I encouraged you to explore your body sensations. But what if you don't like the body sensations that emerge? This is the fourth problem we face: you may avoid being curious to avoid dealing with the feelings that arise.

When approaching a discussion with a "difficult" employee, you might notice butterflies fluttering in your stomach, tightness gripping your muscles, and your heart racing. Remember, these physical manifestations mirror your nervousness, tension, and fear. And while your curiosity propels you through the Infinite Leadership Loop and can guide you toward increased patience, expanded viewpoints, alignment with your moral compass, and stronger relationships, being that vulnerable sometimes sucks!

Let's tackle that last problem first. I teach my clients to use curiosity like a door. You get to choose when to open it and when to close it. You choose how wide you'll open the door, how long you let it stay open, and whether you look through it with open or closed eyes. You don't have to go through it all at once or when you're not ready. However, if you want to grow in certain areas, you will need to get curious about certain things in your past or things that you want to happen in the future, and they won't all be comfortable experiences. Remember you have choice points.

Be aware of raw and open sores, tender spots, and old scars. Often, curiosity takes time. You will open the door a bit but have permission to close it when you've had enough. Let it sit, heal, and then go back to explore further. Over time, you'll learn, discover, and understand more and more about yourself and others.

I struggled when writing *Mastering Confidence*, particularly the section about when things didn't go well for me as a leader. Every time I attempted to write that section, I fell apart. Sometimes, it was so bad that all I could do was sit down and sob. Years after the events of that time, trying to piece together that story again was like reliving the trauma; I had been traumatized by that experience. Yet I knew that I needed to work through it so that I could experience post-traumatic growth.

For me to grow from that traumatic experience, I needed to get curious about what I was feeling as I relived it, which was uncomfortable. Writing about a challenging leadership experience made me feel overwhelmed with emotion. But by staying curious and leaning into the discomfort, I gained new perspectives and insights into my own growth as a leader. Sometimes, though, I wasn't ready for that much emotion, and I'd shut the door of curiosity and try again the next day. Other times, I made space for the intensity of the emotions. Each time, I grew my understanding more and more, which allowed me to unpack the opinions, judgments, and lenses through which I saw that story.

The pivot happened when I could create a new perspective of that time in my life. That story shifted from my old view—that of an incompetent, horrible boss who let her team down. Choosing curiosity allowed me to see a new perspective when I looked back on that time. Transforming pain into awareness, I saw a skilled leader who grew her program immensely thanks to her skills. The consequence of that, though, was that that leader ended up having way too much on her plate, way more than she had the capacity to handle, and as a result fell apart.

By reviewing journals from that time with curiosity, I could see my perspective then, but it was only a piece of the story. I dug deeper, pulling out performance appraisals from those years. Reviewing those helped me see other people's perspectives. Yes, there was a line or two in there about lacking integrity, but there were so many positive comments. There were positive themes in my performance reviews that I had overlooked because I had only been looking at the pain and trauma.

By continuing to be curious, I realized I wasn't the only one who fell victim to that. Overwhelm and burnout are ongoing issues in the nonprofit sector. We continue to push too much onto our leaders without proper training, support, or resources. This new perspective allowed me to see that it wasn't necessarily my fault, and I also realized I needed to take ownership of it. Curiosity not only helped me have a new perspective but also propelled me into action. The new awareness motivated me to proceed forward, finishing the story and the book. Future readers became my purpose for moving forward and teaching the concepts in *Mastering Confidence*.

Now let's look at how to address those problems by shifting our mindset, ditching imposter syndrome, and creating time. Curiosity makes you think differently, helping you take a wider and more expansive perspective and discover new possibilities. Curiosity about how to apply those new ideas moves you forward (to the proceed stage of the loop), and the cycle begins again. Instead of "How do I solve that problem?" you shift to "What would someone acting with integrity do in this situation?"

Curiosity is more than a fleeting interest. It is a mindset. Your view of curiosity has attached to it a collection of beliefs, attitudes, and perspectives that shape how you use curiosity. That is your mindset about curiosity. And it can change. When you pull curiosity out of your toolbox, the willingness to approach a situation with an open mind and a genuine desire to learn and understand has the potential to move you from being stuck to being engaged with an employee. Left in your toolbox, curiosity does nothing for you.

Ask Quality Questions

One of the most powerful parts of curiosity is questioning. We ask questions to know more, understand better, or gain confirmation. Your questions may be related to someone else or to yourself.

There are two guidelines to use when using curiosity as a practice to develop your character:

- Nix "why" questions. They make us defensive and point us backwards.

- Ask forward-facing questions, which generally start with "what" and "how." They open us up and point us forward.

The 80/20 rule of question-asking is a helpful framework for balancing reflection on past experiences with forward-facing inquiry. By spending most of our time focusing on the present moment and the future, we can channel our curiosity toward actionable insights and solutions. About 20 percent of the time, let your curiosity go backwards. Review what happened—the incident or conversation—in your mind or through a self-reflective exercise. Take a nonjudgmental look at the events. Notice when you got triggered and what that trigger was. See how you reacted. A glance back is most likely enough. Now, it's time to shift your focus. A rough guideline for breaking down that 80 percent might be 30 percent on the present and 50 percent on the future. This isn't about exact splits but about intentional focus.

Here are some questions to point you backwards:

- What happened?
- What was I feeling?
- What was I thinking?
- What values were triggered?
- What was going on around me?
- What body sensation did I feel when I was triggered?
- How was my physical, mental, and emotional health at the time?

These kinds of questions help you reflect in the moment:

- What's going on in my body now as I think about this?
- What judgments do I have about how I responded?
- What assumptions do I have about the other person involved?
- What lessons can I take away from this review?

These questions point you to the future:

- What would the person I'm becoming do in a similar situation in the future?
- What strengths can I use to help me be that person?
- What would I need to do to remind myself to use those strengths in the future?
- What do I need to do with my wellness to ensure I'll have the strength of will in those moments?
- What habits do I need to remove?
- What habits do I need to cultivate?

Questions point us in a direction, so craft your questions carefully. The question you ask sends you in search of answers. Therefore, you need to decide on the direction you want to go. Ensure your question points you in the way of progress. I'm not suggesting you ask a question if you already know the answer. A question you don't know the answer to can point you to the other side of figuring it out.

Let's look at an example of self-reflection regarding your team.

What is wrong with this team?

This question leads to finger-pointing shame and embarrassment.

What parts of this team are working well?

This question has the potential to build up and strengthen what is working. Keep going with questions that point you to where you want to go.

What would this team need to do to become our strongest team?

What would I have to do differently to grow my team into the strongest in our organization?

What character traits could I strengthen to grow my team into the strongest in our organization?

Do you feel the power of being intentional about the direction of your questions?

Asking quality questions starts with being mindful and intentional. Think of your questions as your investment. The question you ask affects the answer you get. You must be deliberate in how you craft questions, taking time to refine and change them as you go. If you want an answer that will make a difference in your life, work, and world, find a question that gives you that answer.

Most of us are not conscious of the questions we ask. Instead, a barrage of unconscious queries swirls around in our minds, often seeping out into a voiced rant to whoever will listen in the vicinity.

- What did I do to deserve this?

- When is my life going to change?

- Why can't I do anything right?

- What is wrong with people?

- Why can't they ever get it right?

- When will things ever change?

These questions are unproductive, leading to blame and finger-pointing. They focus on problems and the past instead of solutions and responsibility, leaving you powerless and unable to make changes.

Instead of these victim-based questions, you must ask quality questions that put you back in control. Quality questions produce

Curiosity makes you think differently, helping you take a wider and more expansive perspective and discover new possibilities.

valuable answers that give you something you can do, point you in a direction, and give you hope and optimism. Answering these questions is worthwhile because they move you forward, cultivating your desired character.

Out of the various question starters (who, what, when, where, how, and why), "why" is the one you want to use least, and "what" is the one to use most frequently.

Why do we need to be careful of why questions? When you ask a why question, notice the tone: "Why me?" As we saw above, why questions evoke a victim mentality. When you ask a why question with a victim mindset, you have relinquished all control, giving the power of your thoughts and behaviours to others.

- Why can't anyone ever help me?

- Why do things always go this way?

- Why does this always happen to me?

To quiet the victim mindset, ask better quality questions:

- What belief hinders my ability to ask for help?

- What action will I take today to start better managing my to-do list?

- What thoughts will help me set more effective boundaries and stick to them?

The way to pose why questions is to connect to your bigger purpose and vision in life. These kinds of why questions are not victim statements. Instead, they are profoundly curious questions asked by a person who is consciously developing their character. Here are some examples of effective why questions:

- Why does this matter so much to me?

- Why do I care so much about this project, person, cause, or organization?

- Why is this something I would want to invest my time into?

It's also important to note that a single question may not get you the answer you want or pivot your perspective in the way that helps you become the type of leader you want to be. Instead, a series of well-crafted questions can help you move toward your future vision.

Exploring curiously in this manner becomes the engine that drives the inner work, moves us through the vulnerable in between stage, and gives us the energy to focus on the concrete steps necessary for growth. Questions can ping-pong us back and forth as we gain insight into what's going on internally ("I felt rage") and awareness about the external triggers (a comment). We flip back to what it was about that comment that evoked anger: "What belief do I have? What do I think it said about me?" "Would I have felt the same way if someone else had said it?"

You want to ask yourself a series of questions. Each time you inquire, you move further along the path to your vision and purpose and, of course, to conducting yourself in the manner that aligns with the character you desire. Let me give you an example of how the questions can evolve:

- Why me?

- Why not me?

"Okay, I am the leader. I guess it makes sense that people demand a lot of me. Why can't they at least answer questions for themselves once in a while?"

- Have I encouraged them to figure a solution out before they come to me?

- Have I trained them on how to think for themselves?

- What specific training helps people improve their constructive thinking?

- What could I teach them so they take more initiative in finding answers?

- What company culture would I need to create, or what type of environment would I need to evolve, to make it safe for my employees to brainstorm their own solutions?

- Do I ask them what possible solutions they have come up with when they come to me for help?

- What boundaries might I set to improve this situation?

- What traits would I embody if I was seen as a leader who encourages independent thinking?

- What strong beliefs and values do I have that get in the way of setting firmer boundaries?

- What new ways of thinking would help me see this in a different way?

As you read the questions, you likely shifted from feeling like a victim to feeling curious, empowered, and even excited. Instead of focusing on your employees with bitterness and resentment, you considered what you could do to help them. Perhaps you returned to victim mode when you got to the questions about company culture: "These are all great questions, but I can't change the company culture." Try to ask a couple of quality questions: "What tiny thing could I do that may have a ripple effect in our organization? Who are my allies that might come alongside me with some of those ideas? What would I have to believe about myself to start that ripple effect?"

Calling in curiosity allows you to create the character traits in yourself that create the impact on others you desire. Curiosity is the work of self-reflection, and self-reflection is key to character development.

17

Jot in Your Journal

A S WE MOVE into the fourth practice, a word of caution: if you are not a journal writer, you may have the urge to skip over this section. Don't. It won't serve your growth or the development of your character. Set your resistance to journaling aside for a minute and keep reading. If you are already someone who journals, don't skip over this piece either. There's always more to learn and new ways to journal.

Journaling allows you to take everything you've learned and make sense of it in your own mind. Capturing your thoughts on paper can give you the space you need to see things from a different perspective. Seeing it "in black and white" allows you to mull it over and see what fits with what, what's worth keeping, and what is less relevant. By examining your thoughts through journaling, you can increase your awareness, and you can use this choice point to make decisions, choose behaviours, or plan for triggers. Journaling

- reconnects you to your values
- helps you challenge your assumptions
- realigns you with your desired character
- inspires ideas of how to align with your aspirational identity

Self-reflection is critical to character development; however, inner work is more challenging than one might think. Our logical brain often interferes when we try to peer into our hearts, minds, and souls. We get stuck at the surface level, and sensible reasoning kicks in. We ask, "Why am I so angry?" and answer quickly, "Because he's a jerk, that's why!" We have to train our brains to go deeper and get closer to the core of what is really going on, which takes time and practice, just like athletes practise their physical skills. Journaling gives us a place to practise our mental responses. Take "He's a jerk" a step further: "What thoughts and beliefs do I have that are creating that feeling of anger within me?"

When you can do that deeper dive into your inner workings in the heat of a conflict, you will truly get control of your emotions and reactions and lead with the character you desire. But it takes work to get there, and journaling can help.

When we write freely, we remove the layer of fear, doubt, and judgments about what we should be feeling and the right way to think or act. We gain access to what is, not what should be. It's the ability to see the impact of that thought, idea, or story with a non-judgmental eye.

- Is it helpful?
- Is it true?
- Is it taking me closer to what I desire?

Journaling helps you to clarify thoughts that are jumbled inside you. The hurt you feel about that comment your boss made is mixed up with your grocery list, your mother-in-law's upcoming birthday, and the report you are trying to complete before the deadline. Stress can build in ways we don't realize. As much as you think you're clear on what caused the hurt ("He's a jerk!") and what to do about it ("He needs to back off"), when you can put it down on paper, you find a deeper level of clarity. ("Perhaps he is a bit too direct sometimes, but I'm also sensitive right now because I'm juggling a lot.")

Perhaps you cringe at the thought of journaling. Maybe you've been urged countless times to pick up a pen and start journaling, but it doesn't resonate with you. First, let me assure you this isn't the "Dear diary" kind of journaling. The key is to make journaling work for you, whatever your style. By overcoming your resistance to journaling and spending time in reflection daily, writing becomes a habit, an opportunity for awareness, insight, and increasing our consciousness. We create deliberate time for doing the inner work that later becomes unconscious training we can call on in the heat of the moment; we are facilitating the character development we desire.

Create a daily habit of journaling (and journal whenever you can't figure out what's happening inside you or when faced with a difficult decision). When you do it frequently and habitually—each evening before you go to bed or first thing every day—your mind knows it's coming, and you can let go of putting down the "right" thing on the paper.

Just Write

Notice if you are considering what you are supposed to write as if someone will read it. You might think about word choices and begin to censor them, wondering if you are doing it right. Instead try to write more quickly, letting the ideas flow as they are, without judgment about what shows up. Writing quickly opens up your creative side and frees you from controlling what you are writing. Here are some do's and don'ts that may help:

- Don't look for the perfect scribbler, book, or journal, and don't wait until you find the right pen. Any piece of paper will do.

- Don't worry about neatness. No one, including yourself, ever needs to read this again. You may occasionally want to come back to a great idea you had or review to see how much you've grown, but for the most part, writing has served its purpose once it's down.

- Don't wait for the perfect time. You can journal at the office, on a plane, at the hotel, before a meeting, or while you wait for water to boil or your kids to finish soccer practice.

- Don't wait for the ideal amount of time. Ultimately, you want longer journaling sessions, but one to three minutes of noting thoughts, feelings, and body sensations can still have a huge impact!

- Don't feel obligated to keep what you wrote. Writing shifts our thinking. Feel free to destroy what you wrote, especially if you are worried about it getting into the wrong hands. Sometimes, destroying it can be cathartic.

- Do schedule time in for journaling. Scheduled reflection time is when you pause. You've been so busy doing that you must let your emotions, thoughts, and awareness of your body sensations catch up with you. It's like the snow settling in a snow globe after you've shaken it. You need to give it time to settle.

- Do consider journaling as a practice field. It helps us plan for the future by preparing for how you will show up. You do the practice drills repeatedly, creating new neural pathways as you train your brain. Rehearsing how you might get triggered in an upcoming conversation will prepare you for when you get set off. Journaling is your practice run at managing your emotions. In essence, you are strategizing.

- Do be gentle with yourself. You may worry about the intensity of your writing and what that says about you. I hear you *and* journaling allows us to unpack what is there. It's there anyway. Without unpacking it, it has the potential to hijack us. Journaling increases our emotional intelligence. This is where we learn to name our thoughts and emotions and tame both.

When you unpack the past in your journal, you start to connect the dots. When you piece together a story, you identify triggers, events, beliefs, and roles. It's the dot-connecting that brings awareness to events and emotions. Here's an example of this connection occurring through journaling:

> My admin support is so disorganized. I will have to take some corrective action with her. It's starting to cause some real problems.

Has it always been this way?

Well, no. When I hired her into that position, I appreciated how she was always on top of things and wanted someone to help me with that.

What's happened since she moved into that position?

We picked up that new program. Oh yeah, the team coordinator went on leave, and we haven't replaced her yet. I'm covering a lot of her duties and feeling overwhelmed, so I want my admin to help more. Wait a minute: if I've picked up more, doesn't that mean she's picked up more? We are both overwhelmed and dropping the ball on a few things!

In our journal, we become aware of our current mindset and can examine its effectiveness. In reflection time, we fine-tune our values, clarify our vision, draft our goals, note our successes, and highlight our moments of gratitude.

Alternative Approaches

Here are three alternatives to the free journaling approach.

1. Answer a Question

Start by asking yourself a thought-provoking question related to a challenge or dilemma you're facing. Write down the question at the top of a page and allow yourself to explore multiple answers freely. Here are three questions to get you started:

- What strengths can I leverage here?
- What would the ideal outcome be?
- How can I reframe this situation?

2. Create a Plan

You can use journaling as a proactive approach by crafting a strategic plan. Focus on actions you can take and practical strategies for managing difficult situations. Outlining a clear action plan will equip you

When we write freely, we remove the layer of fear, doubt, and judgments about what we should be feeling and the right way to think or act.

to handle adversity with composure and confidence. To create your plan, follow these prompts:

- The three steps I need to take are...
- The parts of the plan I need to consider are...
- The people involved in this plan are...
- The first step in the plan is...

3. Write Yourself a Memo

Imagine you're advising a colleague or friend facing a similar challenge. Write a memo to yourself offering guidance and insights. By stepping into the mentor role, you tap into your inner wisdom and gain a fresh perspective. You might finish these sentence starters:

- This is what you should consider...
- These are the steps I'd suggest you take...
- Remember to tap into your...

Or you might try a problem/solution framework:

- This is the problem I have:
- Here's what I need to do to fix it:

There is no one right way to journal. Try alternating between these methods to access your inner wisdom and make micro-decisions that align with your values.

Three Character Building Questions

Ultimately, journaling is an opportunity to intentionally develop your aspirational identity. Walk through the three character building questions that shape who you are and how you show up:

1 Embrace your essence: Who am I?
2 Ponder your potential: Who am I becoming?
3 Engage in endless growth: How can I be that now?

I want you to get into the habit of reviewing these questions at a macro and micro level. On a larger scale, you should ponder, journal about, and reflect on these questions as you consider where you are going in the coming years, months, and days. Perhaps even more powerful is applying the three questions on a much smaller scale. The magic happens when you invite these three queries into your thoughts the very instant you feel struggle or tension. When you use these three questions moment to moment to consciously and intentionally shape your conduct, you will find this tool becomes a way of life. In essence, you ask yourself: "Is what I am about to do or say a reflection of who I am and who I am becoming?"

When you sit down on a Saturday morning to journal, you may ask yourself: "Who am I being in my life?" Asking this question on a macro level may make you realize you've been acting scared or timid. You then can make notes in your journal about the kind of person you want to be known as. You could write down, "I want to be seen as a confident person." Pondering how you can *become* more confident, you may consider taking assertiveness training, looking for ways to grow your public speaking abilities, or committing to work out so your body becomes stronger.

Then in the middle of the week when you are at your desk, when your stomach churns and a tension headache comes on a few minutes before a meeting, you can tune in to the work you did in your journal on the weekend. You can go through the same questions, starting with "Who am I being now?" You may realize you are feeling like a victim. You've been taking a "This isn't going to go well" attitude and feel as if you can't change the outcome.

Realizing you are giving away your power, you could ask what kind of person you want to be at this moment. You want to be a confident leader with influence. You can then ask, "How I can be that person right now?" You may remind yourself to evoke a mindset of bravery and courage. You might roll your shoulders back and sit up a little taller, or you might head to the bathroom and power pose before the meeting.

Let's say you want to become a more decisive leader. Right now, you feel wishy-washy about a decision you must make. You reflect on the three questions:

Who am I being? I'm being indecisive.

Who am I becoming? I want to be a responsive decision-maker and feel I can confidently move forward.

How can I be like that now? I can set a deadline for making a final decision and communicate that to my team so they can do their jobs.

Here's another example. When I consider who I want to be as a board member, I answer as an inspirational leader who is caring, encouraging, and straight up in organizational politics. When two executives are acting passive-aggressively with each other and try to use me as a pawn, I need to make some hard decisions about my choice of words and behaviour in the moment. Sometimes, I must bite my tongue and resist the urge to join in the negativity. Sometimes, I must speak up and hold them accountable for their actions.

Who am I now when I choose to engage in gossip? A gossip!

Who do I want to be? A leader with integrity.

What do I need to do right now to be that kind of person? Walk away from the conversation.

Each of these three questions is potent on its own. When combined, they become a tool for leveraging all that you are with all that you are becoming so you can be your best now.

Value-Based Decisions

Use your journal to make value-based decisions. The page is a great place to make decisions that align with your values. Write the decisions, actions, and tasks you plan to take and how they relate to your values.

- What value comes into play here?

- Which of my values is being tested, pushed, or stepped on here?

- Which of my values is being summoned, called forth, or called upon here?

For example, imagine a conflict between two employees that spills into staff meetings with sarcastic comments and death stares across the table. You also know they are leaving each other nasty little notes on the shared communication board in true passive-aggressive fashion.

You know the first employee, Cheryl, the team lead, has been through a messy divorce. You just learned that the second employee, Sasha, who was passed over for the team lead position, is throwing out comments about leaving the organization. She's a good employee who was only passed up for the position because she needed more training and because Cheryl had seniority. You know Sasha would have been better in the position, but you do have protocol to follow. It's a messy situation.

Take a moment to note which of your values come into play. First, write down your top five values. Then circle the top two or three that you feel are most affected here. For example, if you value fairness, that might be one of your values being tugged on here. Perhaps compassion is another, as you notice the challenges Cheryl is facing personally and what Sasha must be going through in being passed over. Notice the thoughts you have:

This isn't fair.

I can't make everyone happy.

What can I do to even things out?

I feel so bad that this is happening.

It's not fair to the rest of the team that they must deal with these squabbles.

You may also be experiencing some anger and frustration.

Why can't these two just grow up?

Life isn't always fair.

It doesn't matter what I do. They will hate me.

Again, consider which values arise with these thoughts. Then consider your possible actions going forward. You could reprimand them both in front of everyone at the staff meeting. That probably isn't the best choice. When you pause and ponder, you'll listen to your body and access your emotional intelligence. You'll be able to ask yourself, "What does my ethical compass tell me to do?" By tuning in to your intuition with thoughtful pondering, you'll come up with an approach that feels authentic to you, sits right in your heart, and will show others that you care about them.

As I've said throughout the book, self-reflection is key to character development. Using your journal as a tool for that self-reflection will give you the clarity and conviction you need to courageously lead with your strength of character.

18

Weave in Wellness

THE FIFTH PRACTICE will shift you from survival mode and give you the emotional stability you crave, the ability to think more clearly, and the enjoyment in leadership and life that you desire.

Here is the problem: constant shallow breathing, chronic fatigue, unhealthy eating habits, lengthy periods of inactivity, and a deadening of your spirit leave you feeling anything but focused on developing your character. If you want to ditch survival mode and conduct yourself in a manner that strengthens your character, you need to move toward thriving. Think about it: you cannot be your best self when you feel crappy. But this shift only happens when you focus on your health and wellness throughout your day in five key domains: breathing, nourishment, movement, rest, and spirit.

When we live in survival mode, we push ourselves to work harder and faster. We are so busy trying to keep up that we don't notice we are in a race we can't win! When we get home at the end of the day, we have less energy for our families, less time to unwind and relax, and fewer hours of sleep. We return to work the next day feeling less rested, less than fully engaged, and less able to focus. The consequence is that we undermine our productivity, our work, and our conduct, which, of course, impacts our character development.

What's more, we are *proud* of being overworked, especially in the nonprofit industry. We boast about the number of hours we work, the number of meetings we have scheduled, and the size of our inboxes. We confuse busyness with productivity and attach our identity to it. How busy you are, the number of meetings you attend, and how late you stay all seem to be related to the quality of your leadership. Yet we know they aren't.

You need to be energized to engage your employees and to feel engaged. Zest, on the VIA Character Strengths profile, often lands at the bottom of most people's charts. Yet zest, or energy and enthusiasm for life, is definitely needed in leadership. But you can't bring it if you don't have it. Too many leaders try to do their best work on a gas tank that is only a quarter full. When the tank empties, they quickly put a bit of gas back in but wonder why they feel depleted again a short time later. Just like your cellphone battery, you need to give yourself a full charge. You need to fill yourself up completely. In a marathon, there are refuelling stations throughout the race. And after the race, runners have days of recovery. Days, not minutes!

Ultimately, we want to feel energized, engaged, and focused when doing our work. This energy gives you the stamina to stick to your boundaries, stretch outside your comfort zone, and share hard but necessary messages. This vitality allows you to be authentic, patient, compassionate, tolerant, regulated, and humble, so you can lead with integrity.

So, how do you do it? I mean, let's face it: you are busy. You have a lot on your plate. There isn't always time to take a break, eat healthily, stretch, or be at one with nature. If you think wellness is an extra, a perk, or a bonus only when you magically have the time, you will never have the time. However, if you shift your mindset to believe that wellness is a prerequisite to strong leadership, you will make the time. In fact, you will prioritize wellness. Setting wellness targets as part of your Character Development Plan can help you regain balance.

The way to add wellness to your workday is to insert micro-moments. A micro-moment of wellness is something you can do in less than three minutes. In the Training Library, I teach a course called Wellness AT Work about the wellness weaved into your day that helps you be your best at work and still have energy for the rest of your life after work. Let's start by looking at the five key components of wellness to focus on.

Breath

The way we breathe tells us whether we are stressed or relaxed. When used correctly, breathing is a tool that can restore tremendous self-control, health, and stamina—all of which are critical for developing character.

Let's say you are working on building your patience. You are at a meeting, and someone says something stupid. Like, really off. Your first instinct might be to look at them and sarcastically ask them if they really just said that. But breathwork can move you away from that snappy comment to patient reflection.

- What did that trigger in me?

- What might be going on for them to make such an outrageous comment?

- What response can I give that is open and curious?

Your breath can help you to cultivate the character trait you desire: patience. There are many forms of breathwork, and I encourage you to search for what feels right for you. I use apps such as Calm or Balance to do guided breathwork as part of my daily meditation practice.

Incorporating any intentional breathing exercise into your workday, even for just a few minutes a day, can yield significant benefits for your overall health and well-being. But there is more to breathwork than doing a breathing exercise. Whether you are in a meeting or sitting alone at your desk, you can use your breath to calm your nervous system in the moment. You might inconspicuously place your hand on your abdomen to help you focus on the breath going in and out. Remind yourself to breathe deeply, rather than shallowly, and channel your ideal self so you can respond in that moment rather than react. Slow your breathing down, and feel it ground you.

Micro-Moments of Breath

Box breathing is a breath technique that involves inhaling for a count of four, holding for four, exhaling for four, and holding again for four, repeating the cycle for relaxation and stress relief.

Alternate nostril breathing involves holding one nostril closed while inhaling through the other, then closing that nostril while exhaling through the first, repeating the process to relax and balance the mind.

You might also keep essential oils in your desk to smell, or you might let out a long sigh to release tension. Like breathwork, these practices will activate your relaxation response.

Nourishment

You need to eat. Okay, that sounds pretty basic, but maybe you tend to forget this. You skip breakfast or have high-carb food, such as a bagel or muffin, when you grab your morning coffee. You pray that it will get you through until you find time to eat again. Lunch comes and goes, and if you're lucky, you'll grab something, but chances are it's two or three before you refuel.

Micro-moments of eating may be all it takes to keep your body budget on track. Certain foods are better at helping you be more productive, have stronger willpower, and have more stamina. What you put in is what you get out, or as I like to say, garbage in, garbage out. Think of eating more healthy protein, fats, and vegetables, and less sugar and carbs.

The motivation here is not to have a slim, sleek body. Focus on the character you want to cultivate. I know it's weird to think about it this way, but the food you put into your body affects the character traits you exude. What you eat is who you are—not physically, but characteristically. If you primarily fuel your body with unhealthy food, you will have a short fuse, short bursts of focus, and much longer periods of scatteredness.

Leadership is an endurance race. You need to keep your body prepared for the long haul! Long days at the office are like long days on the trail. Challenging conversations are like uphill climbs. They literally use the same fuel from your body! Winds coming at you require strong muscles to keep you on course. When you are being hit left and right with challenges, crises, and requests, you need the muscles in your mind to keep you on track. Yes, your brain is a muscle. It accounts for less than 2 percent of your body weight but on average burns 20 percent of your body's energy.

The bottom line is to create micro-moments throughout your day to eat, eat regularly, eat healthy foods, and eat foods that develop muscle because your brain is a big muscle that needs refuelling often.

Micro-Moments of Nourishment

- Have a drink of water.
- Eat a high-protein snack.
- Take a few bites of lunch.
- Eat some veggies or fruit.
- Put your soup in the microwave.

Movement

How often do you get stiff muscles? Maybe a better question is, How often do you notice that you have stiff muscles? In truth, we ignore so much of what goes on in our bodies. We are not tuned in. In fact, we are trying to tune it out. Have you ever put off going to the bathroom? For hours? Don't get me going on how unhealthy that is (think toxins sitting and festering inside of you), but what about how uncomfortable that is? A full bladder. Yes, you can tell me it's not a big deal to you. That is only because you have become desensitized to the uncomfortable feeling. It used to bother you. Over time, you've pushed that feeling away, ignored it, and now you don't even notice it.

Consider the tension in your neck, shoulders, back, or legs. How long is it there or how tight does it get before you notice it? Do you become aware of it only when you stand up and you can't stand up straight? It was there before. Trust me. Again, you just pushed that feeling out of your conscious thoughts. You didn't have time for it.

Movement is critical for effective leadership. Getting stuck in one place physically often means we get stuck mentally and emotionally as well. Micro-moments of movement take us out of stress mode and get us out of tunnel vision. Then we can be more creative, think more strategically, access empathy, and better tune in to our intuition. Moving for even a moment helps us focus better when we return to our work, allowing us to be more productive. The problem is we don't notice we need to move, so we need to create habits and reminders to move. We will talk about that more in the sixth practice: hone your habits.

Micro-Moments of Movement

Think about what you can do in one minute or less to move your body:

- Squats. I've taken up sitting in yogi squat when I need to stretch. This flat-footed squat has oodles of health benefits.

- Stretch your arms and back. Eagle arms is my favourite stretch.

- Drop, roll, or stretch your shoulders. I do this when walking through a door. I put my arms on the door jamb and lean in to get a nice stretch across my chest.

- Jumping jacks, push-ups, or elbows to knees. I was often seen doing my exercises while waiting at the photocopier.

- Walk around inside or go outside for a breath of fresh air. My admin knew I would often go for a walk around the block mid-afternoon.

We confuse busyness with productivity and attach our identity to it.

Rest

It takes a lot of work to keep our bodies on high alert all day, and that is what we are doing. We are prepared, at any moment, to whack the next mole that pops up! Try this: hold your body erect for five minutes. Keep your shoulders back, tummy tight, chin up, and back straight. Keep holding it. Stay tall. Okay, now slouch. Phew. Doesn't the slouch feel good?

The practice of rest is much more than sleep. Rest, renewal, and rejuvenation are all part of the process of helping you maintain your body budget. Our bodies were not meant to be pushed to the degree most of us push them, not just on a daily basis but over the long term. And although we know we should get six to eight hours of sleep a night, most women don't for a variety of reasons. This means we are coming to work sleep-deprived. We need to take rest moments throughout our day to help offset this.

When we rest, we let our bodies, minds, and souls recharge. Why don't we do that? Partly because we've created a culture that suggests resting isn't okay at work. Again, we wear busyness like a badge of honour. You worry you'll be seen as spoiling yourself or being lazy. If you were to take a ten-minute nap at your desk and someone walked in and "caught" you, would you feel as though you had done something wrong? If you try to hide the wellness fundamentals of rest at work, then it might be time to go back and work on your beliefs and mindsets.

Micro-Moments of Rest

When you're feeling fatigued, do the following:

- Sit down if you've been standing for a while.

- Stand up if you've been sitting for a long time.

- Look away or close your eyes and give them a rest from the computer screen every twenty minutes or so.

- Stop the vehicle every hour on long drives to stretch.

- Let your mind rest. Think about something unrelated to work.

- Take a real break!

Spirit

Have you ever felt your heart crushed? What about your spirit? When you feel blah, you are not connected to your spirit. Think of this as just going through the motions at work. You're task-oriented, getting things done, ticking off your to-do list, attending meetings, sending emails—you may as well be a robot. What's more, you tend to feel drained from living in this mode. You've lost your passion for work.

Consider doing those same activities but feeling deeply connected as you do them: engaging in a conversation with a staff member, sending a passion-filled email response, and feeling charged when you leave a meeting. What's different? Somehow, you are more energetic.

That is because there is an energetic component to being connected to your spirit. Spirit is energy in your body. It is the power within. How do you get that feeling? By connecting to and awakening your spirit and understanding what makes it sing—and this might be very individual to you. For some, it's nature, singing, babies, animals, art, spirituality, or gratitude. This practice is about awakening your life force; it's not about spirituality, though if you are a spiritual person, that may come into play.

Why does this matter to your character? Because when you are connected to your core values, the parts of you that matter, you feel a sense of *aliveness*. That's what helps you make ethical decisions to maintain your composure during difficult conversations. The passion in you is engaged.

When you are disconnected from your spirit, you feel dead and disengaged. Your team perceives it as disinterest, indifference, and apathy. You may not say it out loud, but your inner voice is full of "Whatever, I don't care," "I don't give a damn," and "It doesn't matter." You may think it doesn't show, but it does. When you are like this, people don't want to be around you.

When you are connected to your spirit, you feel alive, awake, and engaged. You tend to be more animated with your body and face, smiling, making gestures, and even wanting to dance around. You feel full of life. You are high-spirited. You are engaging, energetic, and enthusiastic. People are drawn to you because of your energy.

Micro-Moments of Spirit

To reconnect to your spirit, you might

- colour or doodle
- meditate
- pray
- listen to music
- tend to your plants
- head out into nature
- connect with clients

Weaving in micro-moments to tend to the five key components of wellness—breath, nourishment, movement, rest, and spirit—will provide you with the fuel you need to build your character, create a magnetic work environment, and have energy left for the rest of your life.

19

Hone Your Habits

THIS FINAL PRACTICE pulls everything together into character development habits. Character is developed in micro-moments, which means you need to hone your habits so that you are much more conscious of how you respond and behave. As a practice to develop your character, we are looking at honing your habits of thinking, acting, and feeling as well as your habits of being.

We all have habits, and the quality of our habits impacts the quality of our lives. We don't usually think about the most important things in our lives, like our legacy, character, and impact on our community. We often don't create habits to cultivate the person we want to be and reach our desired outcome.

You've likely been sitting in survival mode for quite a while. You know it well. It's become a way of life. You have developed damaging habits to cope with lack of sleep, missed meals, and limited time for yourself and your family. You know how to get the critical things done with a hectic schedule at the office, and you have a system in place to ensure you meet everyone's basic needs. These habits are keeping you stuck. We need to remove these habits and install new ones. We have to pull out the weeds before you can plant the seeds!

First, we need to look at what habits you need to eliminate or stop doing. These are the habits that hinder your progress. They might include overthinking, wasting time on social media, making excuses, letting fear stop you, sleeping late, working late, not eating for long stretches, or eating mindlessly.

Second, we need to look at what habits to add or begin. These are the quality habits that move you in the right direction. Several years ago, I wanted more time to do things but couldn't fit them into my day. At some point, I realized that one option would be to get up earlier. Over time (lots of time), I became a 5 a.m. riser, seven days a week. This has given me time for things I always wanted to do but never found the time for. My habits now include yoga, a tapping sequence, meditation, reading, and journaling. The routine is now so habitual that I do it every morning, whether at home, on the road for work, travelling with family, or camping at the lake.

If you habitually book time blocks for deep work, you'll get used to it, as will your employees. When you habitually remind them not to interrupt you and turn them away when they do, you'll get more comfortable with setting boundaries, and they will learn to respect them. When you habitually seek them out after your deep work time block is up to answer their questions, they learn to trust that you care and you follow through. The consistency of the habit makes it work for your team. Suppose you only did it randomly, sometimes allowing interruptions and other times shooing away your employees. You'd never become confident in the process, and those around you would be somewhat confused.

Remember, your daily conduct creates your character. It's not only what you hope to be seen as, wish to emulate, or desire to be remembered for. It is what you *do*—your actions, words, and what you choose not to do. Your behaviour is critical. Your character is defined by who you are moment to moment. As such, you need to be more mindful of who you are moment to moment. Fundamentally, cultivating the character you desire comes from a habit of self-reflection. By monitoring and adjusting your conduct, these habits will help you cultivate your character. Try to do the following:

- Schedule daily reflection time.
- Pause frequently throughout your day.
- Connect throughout your day with who you are and who you are becoming.
- Create time to process hard emotions.

Let's look at each of these habits in depth.

Schedule Daily Reflection Time

When we slow down and reflect, going through the Infinite Leadership Loop, we create a deliberate habit of doing the inner work. This can with time become an unconscious habit. When we ponder and journal, we become aware of our current mindset and examine its effectiveness. As I noted earlier, in reflection time, we fine-tune our values, clarify our vision, draft our goals, note our successes, and highlight our moments of gratitude. During reflection time, we carve out our character, seeing the beauty of who we are and discovering the splendour of who we are becoming.

As I suggested earlier, journaling during your scheduled reflection time can be thought of as practice. You do these drills repeatedly, training your brain to be ready for whatever arises during the "game." You create new neural pathways as you cycle through the Infinite Leadership Loop and ask yourself quality questions. Daily reflection time will help you stay on track with your Character Development Plan.

Pause Frequently

Remember that when we talk about pausing as part of the Infinite Leadership Loop, pause counts twice. You need to pause, or none of the growth work happens. Create a habit of pausing more often.

One way to be more mindful of pausing is to pause before deciding things. These are the choice points we discussed earlier that

**During reflection time,
we carve out our character,**
seeing the beauty of who we are
and discovering the splendour
of who we are becoming.

allow you to regroup before you make decisions. Take a breath, break, or pause. Our automatic reaction is often to make a quick decision or to put it off indefinitely. However, when we create a habit that has us slow down before making a decision, we can become responsive instead of reactive or frozen in time.

I am not suggesting that you think about every single decision each day. I am suggesting you weigh more of the decisions you make, particularly those that relate to your character and leadership.

Connect with Who You Are Becoming

The most powerful way to move forward is to create a habit of connecting with the future vision you have for your character—your aspirational identity. Who you are becoming combines who you already are and what you are cultivating. By connecting with both of these parts, a magnetic pull will help you conduct yourself in a way that moves you toward that vision.

Notice the two parts of what you are connecting to: who you are and who you are becoming. That combines the core of who you are and the extra parts you are moulding. Remind yourself daily of your authentic self, values, beliefs, and strengths. See yourself using these gifts fully. For example, I am a playful, creative, and emotional person. These are characteristics that during professional moments, I often want to shut off. When I connect deeply with who I am, I want to visualize myself using those authentic parts of me. I might see myself gently and playfully teasing my assistant. I may notice how I pull out my Sharpies and a blank piece of paper in front of others to brainstorm. I could visualize myself telling someone I feel frustrated and then describing why, taking responsibility, and discussing our next steps: "I'm frustrated that this part of the project didn't finish. I needed it for today's meeting. I realize I didn't give proper instructions with a deadline, so I will work on more detailed instructions in the future."

In addition to the qualities you like about yourself, consider your darker side that you keep close to your heart. Bringing this side of you into your field of awareness sheds light on it and helps you see the gifts in those parts of you. For example, I have incredibly high expectations of myself. That's good, right? Sometimes. At times, though, I could benefit from increased self-compassion. Those high expectations can also show up as nagging those around me; I might have high expectations of them and push them to do better or demand things outside their zone of potential. Therefore, in reflection time, I could visualize tuning in to others' responses when I check in with them. I could sense their level of comfort and potential with a project. I might ask for their feedback more often: "What would make you feel good and stretched a bit, but not to the point of snapping?" Future visualization allows me to become a character driven leader.

To connect with your aspirational identity, spend time self-reflecting and check in to see if you are aligned with your values and beliefs. That strong connection to your vision lets you chip away at what doesn't belong and carve out the beautiful parts that do.

It's easy to lose sight of your desire to be a certain kind of person. By taking time each day to review what you are working on in terms of your character development and conduct, you will keep it front and centre in your mind.

Determine how it shows up, plan, and role-play. For example, write about an upcoming meeting in your journal during your morning reflection time. You may notice your tendency to get worked up about it. Catching yourself, you remind yourself you are a strong, capable, and knowledgeable woman, equal to anyone else in that meeting. You might reconnect with your passion for the project and your values that are aligned with the project.

Next, consider what could trigger you during the meeting. Perhaps you know there will be someone there who tends to be condescending to you (or others). You may identify the looming deadline and a family vacation coming up and how the two may cause you to be a bit defensive if someone questions your ability (or your team's) to meet the objectives.

Then look at the outcome you desire for the meeting. You want to stay in control of your emotions. You wish to be in integrity, and self-control is one key trait you are working on. Once you have connected with your future vision and identified what might get in the way of that, you can visualize yourself skillfully navigating your way through it. You might feel triggered by a comment, sense yourself tighten, and notice the urge to snap back. Still visualizing yourself in the upcoming meeting, you might observe yourself take a slow deep breath, calm your nerves, and remind yourself of the person you are becoming. You may envision yourself responding in a self-controlled manner, feeling in integrity.

By connecting to who you are becoming, you create a new path in your mind and a new normal way of reacting to situations. You may not remember to do this initially, so create reminders to do this. You can set notifications on your phone, watch, or calendar. You will need regular reminders about what you are working on. When you get the notification and take a moment to reconnect, you may realize you haven't been very patient. Oops. No need to beat yourself up; just get back on track.

Create Time to Process

If you are like most professional women, you don't believe you have time, space, or energy to process everything, so you stuff it down. And then it comes out at the most inopportune times. You probably *don't* have time, space, or energy to do it, but still you *must*.

When you let off steam, it relieves the pressure and helps you be composed. Sometimes, women will tell me they need a good cry, but they can't cry. You need to cry. Crying cleanses your soul, releases past trauma, and enables you to let go of emotional baggage, paving the way for emotional intelligence and inner peace.

You must create a safe time and space to release emotions. Sometimes, I'd do this in the car if I had time to then pull myself together before my meeting. Other times, I'd get up after everyone was in bed or get up early in the morning.

You may need something to trigger the emotional release. Journaling often works for me. I start writing, and I hit a point, a word, a line, or a sentiment that allows the tears to come. Other times, self-compassion works. Self-compassion expert Kristin Neff suggests, "One easy way to care for and comfort yourself when you're feeling badly is to give yourself a supportive touch. Touch activates the care system and the parasympathetic nervous system to help us calm down and feel safe. It may feel awkward or embarrassing at first, but your body doesn't know that. It just responds to the physical gesture of warmth and care, just as a baby responds to being cuddled in its mother's arms."

You can put your hand on your heart, touch your cheek, gently stroke your arms, or give yourself a big hug. Yoga teachers and therapists often use these techniques. Touch can often trigger the emotional release you need.

If you don't release your emotions, you will explode or implode. You cannot continue to let it build and build. Here are some ways to release it:

- Yell in your car.

- Sob in the shower.

- Pour it out into a journal.

- Scream when no one is home.

- Go for a run and pump it out of your body.

- Call your coach, mentor, counsellor, or therapist.

- Talk to a friend, partner, or peer who will let you release it safely.

Here is the thing: developing new habits takes time, and there is a whole science to creating habits. This is why you need to lead with learning. If you struggle to cultivate the habits that will help you lead with your strength of character, you must learn more about habit-building. In the Training Library, I teach strategies for cultivating beneficial habits. Beyond that, I recommend you add books

about building habits to your reading list. You can find a list of rec-
ommended titles at kathyarcher.com/cdlextras.html.

The habit of regular self-reflection leads to a habit of making good
micro-decisions, and that leads to habitually conducting yourself in
a manner that aligns with your aspirational identity. Soon you'll be
the character driven leader you desire to be.

The Power of Leading
with Your Strength
of Character Every Day

'LL SAY IT ONE more time: self-reflection is key to character development. Still, very few women do the work to define their character, create a new vision, and become it. Why do they avoid it? Because the work of exploring who we are and who we want to become is not for the faint of heart. Doing this inner reflection takes us outside our comfort zone. It can be uncomfortable to look at what we are feeling and what beliefs or assumptions have impacted our feelings. It is hard work. It is not always fun. In fact, doing inner work can be downright painful. And it takes time. But it is the only way.

One client told me it's like peeling an onion, and yes, the smell is pungent. Another said, "I don't always like what I find." A third expressed how she shows up differently, depending on her role. "Who am I really then?" she implored with frustration. But each kept going with the inner work.

Our exploration requires us to face and stay with what we find. To let the tears slide down our faces rather than brushing them away. It is necessary to sit with anger and question where it's coming from. We pondering what triggered it and what mistaken belief lies behind it. When sadness overcomes us, we don't always have the time to try to make sense of it. We must make the time, if not now, then later. Similarly, when joy wells up in our throats, we must pause and name it, identifying that this is what we've been searching for. It's been here all along! We were just too busy to notice. We were too overwhelmed trying not to feel anger, hurt, and sadness that we overlooked the joy, happiness, and contentment that were there for the taking.

We must do this work not because it will increase our salary, give us more time, or even make us more competent. We must do it because we want to become our best selves and give that back to the world. No, this isn't always easy work. It requires time, patience, acceptance, curiosity, and a commitment to return to it repeatedly. We need to keep making it a priority.

If you've come this far, it's because you've made the time and a commitment to growing yourself. Congratulate yourself. Not every woman has done what you've just done. Some women were never taught how to do this work and need to learn. Other women do the work to a point but hit a roadblock when they are triggered by a vulnerable point that they are not ready to explore. They then tuck everything away, set aside the journal, and forget about it. And some women used to do it, but they got busy and haven't made it a priority again.

The challenge is that we either face and deal with it consciously or continue to bump up against it unconsciously. We're all guilty of falling off once in a while, but I urge you to keep at it. Sure, we are sometimes triggered and lose it with our staff, boss, or loved ones, and we don't even know where the explosion came from. Our emotions may hijack us, and we react in ways we aren't proud of. We get frustrated with ourselves but can't seem to change things. It's because we never dealt with what's triggering us. So, when you have those bad days, pause, ponder, and find the pivot. Use curiosity to pull you around the Infinite Leadership Loop and do the self-reflective work. We need to get curious about what's causing our unconscious reaction.

Women often stop prioritizing inner work because inner exploration hits a point that hurts. They may have uncovered things they weren't proud of or were ashamed of. Or perhaps they hit a plateau and didn't feel they were making real progress. They didn't see changes in their character. Here's the thing: you can't always see, feel, or even measure the changes in your character. But just like seeds germinating under the soil, we must trust the process. Have faith that something is happening. We must continue to water these seeds and know that something beautiful will grow in the end.

As you move through this journey, you will notice you feel more in control of

- your life
- your work
- your emotions

This is because you will be responsive instead of reactive. When you gain that sense of control, along with it will come the capacity to

- get back into control more quickly when you lose it
- manage your relationships more effectively
- lead authentically and powerfully

Being back in control and feeling capable of doing your job and maintaining emotional stability will cause you to feel aligned—aligned with who you are, with your core values, and most importantly, with your integrity.

Tools in Your Toolbox

As a reminder you have some things in your toolbox now. First, you have the **three character building questions:**

1 Embrace your essence: Who am I?

2 Ponder your potential: Who am I becoming?

3 Engage in endless growth: How am I becoming that?

You have the **five steps for developing your character:**

1 Increase your awareness of how your character develops.

2 Get to know your character strengths and your values, ethics, and morals.

3 Create a vision of your aspirational identity.

4 Create your Character Development Plan.

5 Build a system of ongoing self-reflection with the Infinite Leadership Loop.

The **Infinite Leadership Loop** is your five-step guide for developing character; shaping your own management style; and leading with strong ethics, values, and morals. Remember:

1 Pause: Stop and turn inward.

2 Ponder: Tune in to what is going on inside of you, who you are, and who you are becoming.

3 Pivot: Shift your thoughts, emotions, and intended behaviour.

4 Proceed: Move forward with intention.

5 People: Engage with those around you.

Finally, you have **six practices to make it all stick:**

1 Lead with learning.

2 Call in curiosity.

3 Mould your mindset.

4 Jot in your journal.

5 Weave in wellness.

6 Hone your habits.

This isn't always easy work.
It requires time, patience,
acceptance, curiosity, and
a commitment to
return to it repeatedly.

We follow leaders less because of what they do and more because of who they are. Your character and your reputation guide your people's engagement and their impact. As you've seen throughout this book, it's not so much the things you do but how you do them.

- It's the way you make someone feel when you correct them gently.

- It's the impact you have on your team when you present a new idea.

- It's the kind of person you encourage them to be by being a role model and by mentoring them.

It's about your character.

As we end the book, it's only the beginning of a journey you will be on for the rest of your life, ebbing and flowing around the Infinite Leadership Loop.

I have a few final questions for you. How will you make character building a priority? When will you pause and craft your aspirational identity of who you are becoming? What will your Character Development Plan look like? How will you insert micro-moments of wellness throughout your workday, become more aware of your choice points, and proceed courageously to engage with your people?

I promised you that by the end of this book you would have the tools you need to create your Character Development Plan and to implement it with success. You now have the tools, and implementing them is up to you.

Learning to lead and live with authenticity is a choice. When you choose to do the work, you will return to a feeling of balance more and more often. You will start to reclaim your identity and restore your reputation. By choosing to live your values and live in alignment, you will become a character driven leader.

Congratulations on choosing the path of endless growth toward character driven leadership.

Acknowledgements

THIS BOOK COULD not have been written without my clients. I am deeply grateful that you've allowed me into your lives, your minds, and your hearts. Each time you opened up, shared your stories, and allowed me to ask deep questions, I had the profound privilege of watching you grow and emerge stronger and more aligned. You gave me the opportunity to take what I learned and see it manifested in real life. This was powerful for me and gave me the courage and confidence to write this book. Thank you. For those of you who have told me you are eagerly waiting for my next book: here it is! I appreciate your encouragement and support.

For many, many years, Bill Scott and I met weekly as intellectual partners, challenging each other, sharing ideas, building models, and learning and growing together. Many of the ideas in this book germinated from those conversations. Bill, you championed my work, and our time together built my confidence. Thank you for those Friday calls. Thank you for the rich conversations and for our friendship.

I didn't know the Page Two team existed until one day I noticed that two books on my desk were published by Page Two. I knew right then that they would become my publishers. From my first meeting with Jesse to my work with my editor, Emily, and every single person I've come in contact with since, I've been profoundly grateful to have landed in your care. Thank you, Page Two team!

To the friends who have supported me on this journey, encouraged me, allowed me to check in with certain parts, and cheered me on, thank you from the bottom of my heart. It's been amazing to have you in my corner.

Most importantly, a huge thank you to my family: Ernie, I appreciate your patience and support over the past several years as I kept saying I was going to write another book. Here it finally is. To my children, Jordan, Eric, Amanda, and Leanne, thank you for listening even if you didn't fully understand what I was talking about, for believing in me, and for the feedback. I'm lucky to have a bunch of amazing kids like you all. Thank you to my daughter-in-law Jessica for your support and for keeping an eye out for books I might be interested in and then delivering those books again and again; I am grateful for you and grateful that you work at the library. Thank you!

My five granddaughters inspire me to do this work. I often say that while I'm working to change things for this generation of women leaders, I truly hope we're creating ripples for the next generation of women leaders too. I fully expect that my granddaughters Arriana, Ryleigh, Emerson, Esme, and Paisley will demonstrate leadership in some way, shape, or form in their lives, and I hope that I will have created a positive ripple for each of them. I am grateful for the inspiration I receive from them in my life.

And lastly, I want to acknowledge the role of my faith in my work and in writing this book. Without a deep belief in something greater than myself, I wouldn't be able to do the work that I do. Listening to my clients' stories, supporting each of them through their challenges, and witnessing their pain and joys is profoundly meaningful work. Yet, at times, it can feel heavy. I'm thankful that I never carry this load alone.

My faith has not only guided me as I've taught, coached, and mentored my clients, but also carried me through the writing of this book. When stories were a lot to carry, the task felt overwhelming, or the words seemed elusive, it was my faith that provided the strength and clarity to keep going. It reminded me that this work is not just mine, but part of something much larger. For that, I am deeply grateful.

Appendix: Journaling Prompts

SELF-REFLECTION IS key to character development. Here are questions and journal prompts to help you do the self-reflective work of character development.

Doing the Inner Work

- What are my top three core values?

- What does it look like in my leadership when I am aligned with these core values?

- Thinking back over the last few weeks, when did I struggle to be aligned with these core values? What was happening?

- Looking forward to the future, how can I better honour my values when a similar situation may occur?

- What hills will I die on? Where is my line? What won't I ever do?

- What am I known for? (Not achievements, outcomes, or programs, but the type of person I am)

- What do I think people say about me when I leave the room? Is it what I want them to say?

- What mark do I want to make...

  In my family?
  In my community?
  In this organization?
  In this field of work?
  In the world?

- And why does all of that matter to me?

Tuning In to Your Moral Compass

- What is the ethical dilemma I am facing?

- What actions or behaviours have I not been proud of?

- What does my ethical compass tell me to do?

Reflecting on Your Conduct

- What did I role model for my team today?

- What lessons did my team learn today via my conduct?

- What have I done today to help my team realize their potential?

Connecting to Your Aspirational Identity

If I had the "perfect" life, career, and relationship,

- this is the kind of person I'd be...

- this is what it would look like...

- this is what it would feel like...

- these are the kinds of things that would be happening...

Exploring Character Driven Leadership

- What qualities do I believe are essential for a character driven leader?

- How can I cultivate these qualities in myself?

- In what ways can I demonstrate integrity in my daily actions and decisions?

- How do I handle mistakes and setbacks while maintaining my character?

- What specific actions can I take to build trust within my team and organization?

- How can I use my leadership position to positively influence and inspire others?

Pondering for Growth

- What happened?

- What body sensations did I experience?

- What thoughts were going around my head in terms of beliefs, opinions, and judgments?

- What emotions did I feel as it was happening?

- Which of my values were triggered during this exchange?

- What did I do well in managing that situation? What worked? What didn't work?

- What did I learn?

- How would my best self handle a similar situation in the future?

- What strengths do I need to put to work more often?

Shifting Your Perspective

- If I were advising a friend in my situation, what perspective would I offer them?

- What assumptions am I making about this person or situation?

- If I step back and look at the big picture, how significant is this issue?

Getting Unstuck

- Where am I now?

- Where do I want to be?

- What do I need to do to get there?

- What tiny thing could I do that may have a ripple effect?

- What would I have to believe about myself to start that ripple effect?

Moulding Your Mindset

- What will help me continue to reframe negative thoughts when they occur?

- What thinking patterns no longer serve me?

- What habits will create thoughts that evoke courage in me?

- Is this attitude going to get me where I want to go?

Practising Wellness

- What did I do during my workday today to recharge and refuel?

- Am I consistently getting adequate sleep to support my well-being?

- How physically active was I today?

- When was the last time I completely disconnected from work?

- What dietary habits am I practising to support my energy levels and overall health?

- What am I role modelling about wellness for my staff, clients, community, and family?

Making Decisions

- What kind of decision would the person I'm becoming make? What would the "me at my best" do to lead with my strongest character?

- Do I have time to make this decision?

- Is it someone else's crisis that I am attempting to resolve?

- Do I have enough information to make the decision?

- Have I looked within me to consider how the decision will align with my values, beliefs, and vision?

- Am I avoiding making the decision?

Planning

- The three steps I need to take are . . .

- The parts of the plan I need to consider are . . .

- The people involved in this plan are . . .

- The first step in the plan is . . .

Creating New Habits

- What are my *thinking* habit targets?

- What attitude do I need to cultivate?

- What mindset do I need to come back to on a regular basis?

- What are my *feeling* habit targets?

- What feelings am I aiming for and what feelings do I need to habitually cultivate to get there? How will I do that?

- What are my *action* habit targets?

- What do I need to do daily to stay on the right path?

- What action habits will make me more aware of my choice points so I can think before acting?

Morning Journal Prompts

- What impact do I want to have on others?

- How do I need to show up to have that impact?

- When will I pause during my day?

- What do I need to add to today?

- What do I need to subtract from today?

End-of-Day Journal Prompts

- How did I use my strengths today?

- How did I demonstrate courage today?

- When did my best self show up today?

- What did I learn today that I will apply tomorrow?

To get more journal prompts, head to the *Character Driven Leadership* resource page at kathyarcher.com/cdlextras.html.

Notes

1. Why You Hate Leadership

p. 13 *Gallup research has found:* Jim Clifton and Jim Harter, *It's the Manager* (Gallup Press, 2019), 12.

p. 22 *"we have two options":* Brian Johnson, "+1 or -1 (Which Way Are You Headed?!:)" YouTube, November 18, 2012, youtu.be/s829vll1Jn4.

2. What Does Character Have to Do with It?

p. 33 *Watching Dr. Benjamin Hardy:* Dr. Benjamin Hardy, "The '1-Page Method' to Organize Your Past and Future," YouTube, January 12, 2024, youtu.be/z4HshRqnHeA; Dr. Benjamin Hardy, "Raise Your Floor— The Power of 'Minimum Standards,'" YouTube, June 5, 2023, youtu.be /v8h64ePj-ok.

p. 35 *I read books from authors:* Cheryl Richardson, *The Art of Extreme Self-Care: Transform Your Life One Month at a Time* (Hay House, 2009); Wayne W. Dyer, *Being in Balance: 9 Principles for Creating Habits to Match Your Desires* (Hay House, 2006).

3. What Do Emotions Have to Do with It?

p. 39 *"Emotions are messages":* Joan Borysenko, *Guilt Is the Teacher, Love Is the Lesson* (Warner Books, 1990), 34.

p. 42 *"emotion" is "a conscious mental reaction":* "Emotion," *Merriam-Webster.com Dictionary*, Merriam-Webster, merriam-webster.com/dictionary/emotion.

p. 42 *In* Becoming a Resonant Leader: Annie McKee, Richard Boyatzis, and Frances Johnston, *Becoming a Resonant Leader: Develop Your Emotional Intelligence, Renew Your Relationships, Sustain Your Effectiveness* (Harvard Business Press, 2008), 26.

p. 43 *Psychologist Lisa Feldman Barrett tells us:* Lisa Feldman Barrett, *How Emotions Are Made: The Secret Life of the Brain* (Houghton Mifflin Harcourt, 2017).

p. 43   *If you have "finely tuned feelings":* Lisa Feldman Barrett, "Are You in Despair? That's Good," *The New York Times*, June 3, 2016, nytimes.com /2016/06/05/opinion/sunday/are-you-in-despair-thats-good.html.

p. 43   *As Dr. Daniel Siegel recommends:* Dalai Lama Center for Peace and Education, "Dan Siegel: Name It to Tame It," YouTube, December 8, 2014, youtu.be/ZcDLzppD4Jc.

4. What They Never Taught You About Leadership

p. 48   *Gallup defines engaged employees:* "What Is Employee Engagement and How Do You Improve It?" Gallup Work-place, gallup.com/workplace /285674/improve-employee-engagement-workplace.aspx.

p. 48   *Employee engagement reflects:* Jim Harter, "3 Key Insights into the Global Workplace," Gallup Workplace, June 12, 2024, gallup.com /workplace/645416/key-insights-global-workplace.aspx.

p. 54   *"Your brain's main job":* The University of Waikato, "'How Emotions Are Made: The Secret Life of the Brain'—Dr Lisa Feldman Barrett," YouTube, October 13, 2020, youtu.be/KliA19umFyY.

p. 58   *One of the twelve statements:* "How to Measure Employee Engagement with the Q12®," Gallup Workplace, gallup.com/workplace/356045 /q12-question-summary.aspx.

p. 59   *The number one question:* "Gallup's Employee Engagement Survey: Ask the Right Questions with the Q12® Survey," Gallup Workplace, gallup.com/q12.

5. Developing Character Awareness and Essential Leadership Traits

p. 68   *Overusing honesty could mean:* "Finding the Golden Mean," VIA Institute on Character, viacharacter.org/pdf/GoldenMean.pdf.

p. 69   *Aristotle says:* Garth Kemerling, "Aristotle: Ethics and the Virtues," The Philosophy Pages, philosophypages.com/hy/2s.htm.

p. 74   *as Neale Donald Walsch says:* Neale Donald Walsch, *Conversations with God: An Uncommon Dialogue—Book 3* (G.P. Putnam's Sons, 1998), 331.

p. 76   *Physical courage as defined by Olivier Serrat:* Olivier Serrat, "Moral Courage in Organizations," *Knowledge Solutions* 103 (June 2011): 1, ecommons.cornell.edu/server/api/core/bitstreams/671f5b43-cf9d -4a1b-aa3d-d85910c995d0/content.

p. 76   *Serrat defines moral courage as:* Serrat, "Moral Courage," 1.

p. 77   *Michael Josephson, who founded:* Michael Josephson, "Moral Courage— The Engine of Integrity," *What Will Matter* (blog), November 2011, whatwillmatter.com/2011/11/commentary-moral-courage-the -engine-of-integrity.

p. 78   *hope theory developed by Charles R. Snyder:* C.R. Snyder, Kevin L. Rand, and David R. Sigmon, "Hope Theory: A Member of the Positive Psychology Family," in *The Oxford Handbook of Hope*, edited by Matthew W. Gallagher and Shane J. Lopez (Oxford Academic, 2017): 27–44, doi.org/10.1093/oxfordhb/9780199399314.013.3.

6. Who Are You, and Who Are You Becoming?

p. 84   *Author and commentator David Brooks:* David Brooks, *How to Know a Person: The Art of Seeing Others Deeply and Being Deeply Seen* (Random House, 2023), 64.

p. 84   *VIA Character Strengths:* You'll find the VIA Character Strengths profile at viacharacter.org/character-strengths. See also Dr. Ryan Niemiec, "What Are Your Signature Strengths?" VIA Institute on Character, viacharacter.org/topics/articles/what-are-your-signature-strengths.

p. 84   *also do the CliftonStrengths assessment:* You'll find the CliftonStrengths assessment at gallup.com/cliftonstrengths/en/252137/home.aspx.

p. 85   *several self-reflective exercises:* You can learn more about my Values Verification course here: kathyarcher.com/values.html.

p. 91   *Dr. Benjamin Hardy reminds us:* Benjamin Hardy, *Personality Isn't Permanent: Break Free from Self-Limiting Beliefs and Rewrite Your Story* (Portfolio, 2020), 113.

p. 91   *As Dr. Benjamin Hardy says:* Hardy, *Personality Isn't Permanent*, 109.

p. 91   *"Trauma is not what happens to us":* Gabor Maté, "Foreword," *In an Unspoken Voice* (North Atlantic Books, 2010), xii.

p. 92   *Even though we long thought:* Mathew A. Harris, Caroline E. Brett, Wendy Johnson, and Ian J. Deary, "Personality Stability from Age 14 to Age 77 Years," *Psychology and Aging* 31, no. 8 (December 2016): 862–874, doi.org/10.1037%2Fpag0000133.

p. 92   *"Your goals shape your identity":* Hardy, *Personality Isn't Permanent*, 109.

7. Create Your Character Development Plan

p. 104   *procrastination or motivation equals expectancy:* Brian Johnson, "*The Procrastination Equation* by Piers Steel," YouTube, August 20, 2015, youtu.be/I3GqcZJdswo.

p. 107   *Learn more about leadership competencies:* To learn about leadership competencies, listen to "Episode #24: Overlooked Leadership Competencies You Need to Pay Attention To!" *Surviving to Thriving with Kathy Archer*, podcast, kathyarcher.com/podcast/24.

9. Pause

p. 133   *the Calm or Balance meditation app:* You can find the Calm app at calm.com and the Balance app at balanceapp.com.

10. Ponder

p. 145   *"You can point with the sword of truth":* Anne Lamott, *Bird by Bird: Some Instructions on Writing and Life* (Pantheon Books, 1994), 156.

11. Pivot

p. 154   *"the skill of being fluid and adaptive":* Hardy, *Personality Isn't Permanent*, 49.

p. 155   *"You feel what your brain believes":* Feldman Barrett, *How Emotions Are Made*, 78.

p. 156   *"[you] respond to what you perceive":* Helen Schucman, *A Course in Miracles* (Viking: The Foundation for Inner Peace, 1976), 11.

p. 160   *Brené Brown encourages us:* Brené Brown, *Rising Strong: The Reckoning, The Rumble, The Revolution* (Spiegel & Grau, 2015), 86.

12. Proceed and People

p. 167   *the character strengths associated with courage:* "The 24 Character Strengths: Courage," VIA Institute on Character, viacharacter.org /character-strengths.

14. Lead with Learning

p. 191   *Cal Newport's book* Deep Work: Cal Newport, *Deep Work: Rules for Focused Success in a Distracted World* (Grand Central Publishing, 2016).

p. 191   *Mental performance coach Brian Cain:* Brian Cain, "One Percent Better: How to Intentionally Invest into Yourself So You Can Invest Your Best into Others," online keynote address, May 6, 2022, briancain.com /portage.

p. 194   *I learned a lot about character:* Eleanor Roosevelt, *You Learn by Living: Eleven Keys for a More Fulfilling Life* (Harper & Brothers, 1960); C.S. Lewis, *The Screwtape Letters* (Geoffrey Bles, 1942); and C.S. Lewis, *Mere Christianity* (HarperOne, 1952).

p. 194   *I'm often learning from historical figures:* Ryan Holiday is a key source of my insights on Stoicism. Find his books and videos at ryanholiday.net.

p. 194   *our emotions are predictions:* Feldman Barrett, *How Emotions Are Made*, 69.

p. 194   *insight into developing character:* Rick Warren, *The Purpose Driven Life: What on Earth Am I Here For?* (Zondervan, 2002).

p. 194   *"impossible to change your past":* Lisa Feldman Barrett, "Your Brain Predicts (Almost) Everything You Do," *Seven and a Half Lessons About the Brain* (Houghton Mifflin Harcourt, 2020).

15. Mould Your Mindset

p. 198   *how emotions are constructed:* Flow, "How Emotions Are Made (Cinematic Lecture)," YouTube, April 14, 2020, youtu.be/0rbyC5m5571.

p. 200   *Rumination teaches your body:* Feldman Barrett, *How Emotions Are Made,* 183.

p. 200   *the authors describe your internal operating system as:* Robert J. Anderson and William A. Adams, *Scaling Leadership: Building Organizational Capability and Capacity to Create Outcomes That Matter Most* (Wiley, 2019), 8.

18. Weave in Wellness

p. 232   *Zest, on the* VIA *Character Strengths profile:* Robert E. McGrath, "Character Strengths in 75 Nations: An Update," *The Journal of Positive Psychology* 10, no. 1 (July 2014): 41–52, dx.doi.org/10.1080/17439760 .2014.888580.

p. 235   *less than 2 percent of your body weight:* Markham Heid, "Does Thinking Burn Calories? Here's What the Science Says," *Time,* September 19, 2018, time.com/5400025/does-thinking-burn-calories.

19. Hone Your Habits

p. 248   *"give yourself a supportive touch":* Kristin Neff, "Exercise 4: Supportive Touch," Self-Compassion, self-compassion.org/exercises/exercise -4-supportive-touch.

About the Author

KATHY ARCHER used to be a nonprofit leader overwhelmed by her role and responsibilities. Thankfully, she turned that around! Kathy lives with her husband and walking partner, Max, a golden retriever. Their kids and five granddaughters are frequent visitors, bringing lots of fun. Kathy reads extensively, crochets, and enjoys puttering with her gardens and houseplants.

No One Should Have to Do Leadership Alone!

Take the Next Step in Your Leadership Journey

Are you feeling inspired by the insights in this book? You've gained valuable knowledge. Now it's time to put it into action. Join the Training Library, my membership program designed to provide ongoing training, coaching, and support to lead confidently and authentically.

Membership includes a personal library of leadership training courses and worksheets, monthly live group sessions with me, and community support with vibrant women leaders also on their leadership journeys. It also includes practical tools, like downloadable resources to implement immediately.

Join the monthly membership and

- become confident in your leadership abilities
- bounce back when adversity hits
- be your best self
- find a place to belong

Visit kathyarcher.com/library and start your transformation today.

Unlock Your Aspirational Identity!

You can also try my accelerated program for a more immersive experience. In the six-month Character Driven Leadership program, you'll receive personalized one-on-one coaching, monthly group calls, and peer mentoring to fully apply the book's principles to your life. Designed for those who are serious about deep, transformational growth, this program offers extensive support and guidance. Ready to go all in? Discover the Character Driven Leadership program at kathyarcher.com/character-driven-leadership.html.

Bring Me into Your Organization

Amazing teams bring me into their organization virtually to teach strength-based leadership—from a lunch-and-learn session to a year of ongoing training. Let's talk about how to help your leadership team thrive and lead with authenticity.

Create a book club with your peers and go through *Character Driven Leadership* together. Do it on your own or let me guide you through the book.

To talk about these options, reach out to me at kathy@silverrivercoaching.com.

Stay Connected

I *love* hearing from students, clients, and readers. Reach out to me on any of the socials. My favourite place to hang out is Instagram. And you'll find a popular weekly newsletter on my LinkedIn. I'm easy to find: @kathydarcher on all socials.

KATHYDARCHER

www.ingramcontent.com/pod-product-compliance
Lightning Source LLC
Chambersburg PA
CBHW030456210326
41597CB00013B/685